Praise For

THE CONSUMMATE LEADER

"While most leadership books err on the side of syrupy platitudes or dusty research, Patricia Thompson's *The Consummate Leader* is that rare combination of practical wisdom filled with heart. I am confident that the principles contained in this book can be of immediate benefit to leaders at all levels if they are considered and applied in the way outlined by Dr. Thompson."

—Daniel Crosby, PhD,
President, IncBlot

"In the conversationally written *The Consummate Leader*, Thompson effectively underscores the importance of leaders knowing themselves deeply, being guided by meaning and purpose, connecting with others in an authentic fashion, maintaining a positive outlook, sharing their perspectives in a genuine manner, and mentoring and coaching others. This book integrates real-world examples with relevant science in a way that encourages and supports individuals to enhance their leadership competence. The author's approach to leadership is refreshing and very humanistic and will appeal to individuals wanting to begin a career in leadership, as well as those with considerable leadership experience."

—Nadine J. Kaslow, PhD, ABPP
2014 President, American Psychological Association
Professor and Vice Chair, Emory University School of Medicine

"True leadership results in capturing the hearts and minds of others. Patricia Thompson's *The Consummate Leader* provides leaders with the tools to achieve this feat. This book represents wisdom in theory and practice, and inspires leaders to reach for the balance and joy that accompanies deeper self-knowledge. I consider this a must-read for those who aspire to not simply be leaders, but to be luminaries for others."

—Karen Watts
Chief Nursing Officer, Northeast Georgia Health System

"*The Consummate Leader* is different from the many other leadership books I have come across. It not only provides you with actionable strategies to improve professionally, it also causes you to take a long hard look at yourself to grow on a personal level. I highly recommend it."

—Joslyn Gordon,
Chief Engineer, Lynk Systems

"In *The Consummate Leader,* Patricia Thompson masterfully blends psychology, spirituality, and the science behind effective leadership, presenting evidence and posing questions that really make you stop and think. Having served as an evangelist for over two decades and currently championing emotional intelligence in the workplace, I find this book to be an invaluable resource. Embrace the lessons contained within its pages, and you will elevate the way you lead and live."

—Richard Hua
Senior Sales Consultant and Technical Architect, Oracle

"Patricia has wonderful insights into how self-awareness, self-management, a positive attitude, and excellent relationship skills can be used effectively in an organization. She makes a strong case that her seven key characteristics found in consummate leaders can be developed, but she also emphasizes that personal development takes discipline, self-monitoring, practice, and feedback. This is a wonderful guide for personal growth."

—Barry Blakley, PhD, M.Div.
Minister of Hopewell United Methodist Church, Gainesville, GA

"*The Consummate Leader* is a book that is applicable to leaders in a variety of fields. Identifying work that is truly meaningful to you, connecting with others in an authentic way, and skillfully coaching and mentoring are invaluable skills that can benefit all people in positions of influence. Whether you aspire to leadership or are already directing others, Thompson's *The Consummate Leader* will help you enhance your skills."

—Ron Kellman, President & CEO
Sports Tourism International and Sports Horizons Group, Inc.

"Dr. Patricia Thompson's *The Consummate Leader* is a hugely refreshing read! It is a wonderful balance of the theoretical and the practical. She outlines exercises and explanations of the 'key' to each and shows how best to pull it all together – with a clear, straightforward, and at times conversational writing style. She lays out a credible roadmap for personal and professional development and shows the reader how to be leaders in both areas. What's more, she is generous in sharing her own experiences and journey of self-exploration. Her passion for and love of her work jumps off each page, and her holistic approach gives the reader thoughts for reflection right away. This book is a gift!"

—Patricia Masters Daniels
Retired Global HR Operations Leader
Mercer (a Marsh & McLennan Company)

"This is not your everyday HOW TO. Thompson, with her wit, experience, and knowledge, manages to gently coerce the reader to better him/herself through exercises, encouragement, and common sense. By sharing her personal experiences, failures, and success stories – as well as those of numerous people she has helped in her brilliant career – she opens a door that many fear is closed. She remains true to her core beliefs and yet doesn't preach. Her anecdotes resonate and her message is clear: set a goal, work hard at reaching it, and the results will follow. Above all, she reminds us of our humanity; though we may fail, there are various ways to measure success. And through it all, the reader is encouraged to push and work at achieving a higher state of being. No matter who we are or what our goals may be, we are encouraged to strive to be the best we can be: as the consummate leader – and even the consummate self."

—Daniel Beauchemin
Global Management and Corporate Image Design Consultant
Co-Founder, MPA Art Consultancy

THE CONSUMMATE LEADER

Copyright © 2014 Patricia Thompson

All Rights Reserved. No part of this book may be reproduced in any form or by any means, electronic or mechanical, including photocopying, recording, or by any information storage and retrieval system, without permission in writing from the author and publisher.

All names used in this book have been changed to protect the privacy of those referenced.

SpongeBob Squarepants is a registered trademark of Viacom International Inc.

ISBN: 978-0-9960479-1-3

Published by
Silver Lining Psychology
Atlanta, GA

Editing and book design by Stacey Aaronson

Printed in the USA

THE CONSUMMATE LEADER

A Holistic Guide to Inspiring Growth in Others ... and in Yourself

PATRICIA THOMPSON, PhD

This book is dedicated to Eva and Lloyd Thompson,
who have always supported me in following my dreams.

It is also dedicated to Markeal, who has been ~~harassing~~
encouraging me to write a book for years, and to Blake, with love.

consummate

adjective | ˈkänsəmət |

Carried to the utmost extent or degree; of the highest quality; complete; perfect; showing a high degree of skill and flair.

Table of Contents

Foreword	1
Introduction	3
Chapter 1: The Consummate Leader	**7**
What Is a Consummate Leader?	10
Characteristics of a Consummate Leader	12
How to Use This Book	15
Chapter 2: Self-Awareness	**17**
Trucking Along	21
How to Become More Self-Aware	22
Going Deeper	31
Tell Me about Your Childhood ...	32
Chapter 3: Spirituality	**42**
What Is Spirituality?	44
What's It All for Anyhow?	46
What's My Motivation?	49
Ebenezer Scrooge and Leadership	53
Helping Others to Find Meaning	55
My Story	57
Chapter 4: Self-Management	**64**
Mind Control	66
I Think I Can, I Think I Can	76
Lessons from SpongeBob SquarePants	79
Calgon, Take Me Away!	86
Ready, Set, Go!	93

Chapter 5: Positivity — 96

- Positive Leadership — 98
- Come On, Get Happy! — 99
- Joy to the World — 100
- A Formula for Happiness — 105
- Happiness Toolbox — 107
- Purposefully Set a Positive Tone — 120

Chapter 6: Authenticity — 123

- Is It Safe to Be Authentic? — 127
- Who Do You Want to Be? — 130
- Give Me an "M"! Give Me an "E"! — 132
- Strike a Pose — 135

Chapter 7: Positive Relationships — 142

- No Man Is an Island — 144
- What's Love Got to Do with It? — 146
- You Can't Hurry Love — 150
- Strategies for Building Relationships — 152

Chapter 8: Coaching and Developing — 161

- Where Are You Going? — 165
- Channel Your Inner Cher Horowitz — 167
- Getting to Know You — 171
- The Other F-Word — 177
- One Size Doesn't Fit All — 185

Chapter 9: Pulling It All Together — 189

Appendix: List of Strengths — 195
End Notes — 197
Recommended Reading & Viewing — 209

FOREWORD

In the aftermath of the dot-com crash, I found myself at a crossroads. I was a failed entrepreneur whose dreams of wealth and fame had evaporated along with the NASDAQ; I was also a young father who was worried that my lack of financial success had let down my wife and kids. Worst of all, I wasn't sure who I was. I had been proud, even arrogant, when looking back over what seemed like an unbroken string of academic and professional success. I measured myself based on my bank account, news articles, and awards. Now, I wasn't sure what to think.

Fortunately, for my happiness and my career, it was then that I discovered the teachings of positive psychology. As I read the works of pioneers like Martin Seligman and Edward Deci, I discovered that other people had researched my pathologies and challenges and had found authentic, proven ways to be happier and more productive.

By applying the principles of positive psychology to my own life, I became a better husband, father, and businessman. Not only did my life become happier and more meaningful, I also became more "successful" in the eyes of the world after starting several more companies and helping dozens of my fellow entrepreneurs as an investor and advisor.

When other people asked me to share the secrets that brought me success and happiness, I would provide them with a long reading list of essential works like Mihaly Csikszentmihalyi's *Flow* and Carol Dweck's *Mindset*. I even prepared a 43-slide presentation that laid out the lessons I'd learned. But what I really wanted was a single book that would encapsulate the principles that had so improved my life, specifically aimed at a market of business professionals.

Selfishly, I had hoped to write that book myself someday. But when Patricia shared *The Consummate Leader* with me, I realized that she had already written it – and had done a far better job of conveying the key ideas than I could have done.

With wisdom, humor, and grace, Patricia has written a book that should be an essential part of any leader's bookshelf. Not only does she explain the principles of authentic leadership in a clear, concise way, she also provides detailed, concrete stories that illustrate these principles, both from her own life and from her practice as a corporate psychologist.

The Consummate Leader is not merely an inspirational read (though it certainly delivers in that regard); each chapter includes specific tools and exercises to help you discover insights into your particular situation and circumstances. Whether you're a young leader starting out in your career or a self-styled management expert like me, this book can help you improve your leadership skills, your business performance, and your life.

The Consummate Leader is an important work that deserves to have a major impact on today's workplace. I'll be sharing it with all the leaders I work with … and once you finish it, I suspect you'll do the same.

—Chris Yeh
Entrepreneur, Investor, and Co-Author of
The Alliance: Managing Talent in the Networked Age

INTRODUCTION

This may be the world's only leadership book for which the genesis was a breakup (or for which the author actually *admits* that its genesis was a breakup). In early 2009, a relationship I had thought would turn into happily-ever-after turned into miserably-no-longer-to-be. At the time, I was five years into my current career as a management consultant (and happened to have a PhD in Clinical Psychology), so I had the benefit of years of training and education in constructive strategies to deal with this unexpected change of affairs.

I exercised (when I could drag myself away from marathons of *Love Actually,* *The English Patient,* and *Before Sunrise*), made time to socialize with friends (when I wasn't taking preposterously long naps and single-handedly increasing Kleenex's stock value), read self-help books (when I wasn't blowing unconscionable amounts of money on my newly acquired purse fetish), and wrote in my journal (in which I penned unfit-for-print entries about my ex).

After a few weeks of alternating between the productive and ridiculous, I eventually reached the conclusion that I should probably begin putting some of my self-help readings and graduate school training into practice in order to gain some perspective and move on from the experience. Yes, my ex had engaged in some blameworthy behavior, but I didn't want to continue to focus on that. Instead, I decided to use the occasion to take a hard look at myself, better understand my role in the proceedings, and gain greater self-awareness. I figured that if I actually walked away from the experience having acquired some sort of life lesson, I could prevent myself from becoming bitter, and actually become a better person for having gone through it.

So, looking at myself deeply is exactly what I did. I engaged in a period of self-reflection (that continues to this day), so that I could more fully understand myself. I decided to take on an attitude of "radical self-responsibility" (as Claire Zammit and Katherine Woodward-Thomas call it) so that I could work on controlling the one thing over which I had control – myself.

After reflecting on the relationship, I decided to focus more broadly on my interactions with others. Instead of focusing outward when someone behaved in a way I didn't like or when some disappointment occurred, I made a practice of looking at the role I played in the situation. If the same scenario seemed to be playing itself out over and over again, I chose not to curse the unfairness of the world, but instead to see how I contributed to repeating patterns as the common denominator. In this way, I was better able to monitor my reactions to events that arose in my life, and as you might expect, ended up breaking patterns and creating more positive outcomes.

I also focused on spirituality – meditating regularly, looking for meaning in the events that happened to me, and being truly grateful for the many positive aspects of my life. Across time, all this self-reflection created even more positive outcomes: I lost weight, increased my energy, and improved my confidence. And, as luck (or self-responsibility) would have it, about six months after the breakup with said ex and all the ensuing work on myself, I began dating my now-husband.

Now I'm sure that as many of you read this you may be thinking, "Well that's all well and good, and I'm glad you're now healthier and paired off, but when I picked up this book, I was expecting information on leadership. So, excuse me for asking, but what does all of this have to do with becoming a more effective leader of people?"

Quite a bit, actually. While I was doing all of this work on myself, an interesting side effect was that my efficacy working with others increased. Before all of this occurred, I would say I was a good executive coach and consultant who helped people to work toward their goals. However, after my self-development journey, I noticed I was able to help people even more effectively.

Having a deeper understanding of myself increased my ability to monitor my reactions to others' behaviors and to use that data to inform my work with them. Further, by checking in with myself more regularly, I was able to connect with others in a way that I had not previously been able to do. My empathy and ability to stay present with others increased, as did my facility in helping them to capitalize on their strengths, reach within, and make changes that may have been challenging for them. By going through a process of better understanding myself, I was able to better understand others – and help them to understand and develop themselves.

As a management consultant, I have come across a lot of books geared toward helping people to become more effective managers and leaders. There are books on how to manage change, how to delegate, how to be more organized, and how to hold people accountable; books on managing talent, influencing others, and presenting in the most effective manner. I have found these to be wonderful resources for myself and my clients; however, one thing I have found lacking is that there are not enough books that encourage the reader to take the kind of deep, hard look at himself[*] required to maximize his personal and professional development. It is one thing to apply a behavioral technique, and quite another to connect with others in such a way that the technique becomes secondary. This book is my attempt to fill that gap.

Lest you think you do not need this book because you are already highly effective, or perhaps too old a dog to be taught new tricks, I encourage you to suspend your disbelief for the moment and continue reading. For example, I have come across some clients who have asserted to me, "I'm 55 years old. I've always been this way, so that's the way I'm always going to be." I'm sorry to offend you if you're one of those people, but I believe this sort of reasoning is a cop-out. From experience, I know that we are never "fully cooked" unless we believe we are.

As the psychologist Karen Horney stated: "There is no good reason why we should not develop and change until the last day we live." By engaging in the regular habit of looking within and striving to better ourselves, we can continue to grow by leaps and bounds. It is my sincere hope that by reading this book and completing the exercises within it, you too will be able to have new insights and breakthroughs that will lead to greater accomplishments and contributions as a leader, both at work and in your personal life.

Freedom is man's capacity to take a hand in his own development. It is our capacity to mold ourselves.

—ROLLO MAY

---

[*] I will be alternating between using the masculine and feminine pronouns for ease of readability.

CHAPTER ONE

THE CONSUMMATE LEADER

Out of all the leaders with whom I have had the pleasure to work, one of the most inspirational ones is a woman named Grace.† I first met Grace in my role as a corporate psychologist when I was assessing her for a position as an office leader for a Fortune 500 global consulting firm. From the moment we first started chatting, I found myself drawn to her – aside from an undeniable charisma and presence, she had the sort of infectious and upbeat personality that puts others at ease and encourages connection.

Grace was smart, mature, collaborative, and driven. She was someone who set aggressive goals and was willing to put in the time and effort to achieve them; she knew her strengths

---

† Names and some details have been changed to ensure individuals' confidentiality.

and areas for development and was very open about them. She was making efforts to improve in the areas that needed to be addressed, but she was incredibly undefended when talking about them, as she was aware that sharing with others was the best means to receive further feedback to help her grow. As you may expect, Grace impressed everyone throughout the interview process and was enthusiastically hired.

Once she began working with the firm, however, things did not proceed as she had hoped. Part of the reason Grace had been brought into the organization was to leverage her creativity and entrepreneurial spirit to drive organizational change. However, as anyone who is attempting to transform a culture knows, it is a process that takes time and is often met with resistance. Grace experienced the frustration associated with coming into a new workplace with big dreams and goals, only to find out that the organization's readiness for change was not what she had anticipated. Like a lot of driven people, she had hoped that results would come immediately. So, when this did not happen, she was understandably disappointed.

To her credit, she recognized her frustration and knew that if she wasn't careful, she would become disillusioned, and so she took various steps to take care of herself during that time. She knew that to be effective, she had to prevent herself from burning out by managing her stress and focusing on controlling the things over which she had control. She hired a like-minded individual to be an ally in the office to help with achieving her objectives, socialized with friends to ensure she got the support she needed, engaged in her hobbies when she was able to do so, and stayed focused on her reasons for selecting her chosen career path when things became particularly difficult.

Despite some of the resistance she faced, Grace had a strong sense of belief that her vision for the office was one that would help them to be more financially profitable. So, with her confidence and optimism intact, she purposefully went through a process of planting seeds to gain buy-in for her ideas.

Because she was an outstanding relationship builder, she was intentional about establishing and maintaining relationships with client prospects and colleagues throughout the firm. She balanced her desire to persuade with a genuine spirit of openness, which allowed her to better understand the people she was hoping to influence. When others observed her success in securing meetings with prospective clients, they were curious to know how she was accomplishing feats that others had previously been unable to do. As a result, she started to get pulled into various meetings and corporate initiatives, which further enhanced her visibility and ability to influence.

The people in her office appreciated Grace's upbeat spirit, strategic thinking skills, and participative management style. She focused on mentoring and developing people, and as a result, the junior people who worked with her had the sense that she sincerely cared about them and their careers. While her lighthearted and sometimes irreverent style was quite different from approaches to which they had become accustomed, they were inspired by her vision for the future. They saw the success she was having in positioning herself within the firm, and they were intrigued to see if she could garner more corporate resources for their relatively small office.

As I worked with her over time, it was clear that although Grace cared about people a great deal and had wonderful interpersonal skills, she was anything but a pushover. In fact, she was frequently the only person in the room who was willing to appropriately challenge others' perspectives or make a potentially unpopular comment. She would "call a spade a spade" or pleasantly push back in response to unreasonable bureaucratic demands. However, because she had effectively built relationships and was clearly coming from a position of wanting to do what was best for the firm (as opposed to political wrangling), her assertiveness and contributions were well respected by others.

At the time of this writing, the outcome of Grace's story at this particular organization is still to be determined. She is still planting seeds and gradually coaxing people around her to move toward the sort of culture they had originally stated they desired. However, in the relatively short time she has been there, she has been identified as a valued employee who is perceived as having the potential to make a significant impact within the company.

Grace has given herself a reasonable timeline for effecting the changes she believes will move her office in the desired direction. At that point, she will reassess whether she believes the company's culture is a good fit for her and evaluate whether or not it will provide her with the sort of meaning and purpose in her career that she needs to maintain a sense of fulfillment. In the meantime, she soldiers on, pursuing her goals with a dogged sense of determination.

WHAT IS A CONSUMMATE LEADER?

I share Grace's story because she is the epitome of a consummate leader, an individual who knows herself deeply and is comfortable in her own skin. She realizes, as all of us should, that she is a work in progress who has (and always will have) opportunities for further growth and development. In fact, unlike many people I have assessed who listen to the feedback I present during a follow-up session and move on from that session without making much of an effort to integrate it into their work lives, she proactively asked if we could periodically check in with one another to discuss her experiences at the firm and explore ways to increase her effectiveness.

Grace takes a holistic approach to life and leadership – she understands that to be at her best in a work environment, she likewise needs to be at her best in her life in general. In contrast to most clients who dig in and put in more effort and hours when faced with work stress, she knows that she has to get a handle on her stress and work *smarter*, as opposed to *harder*. Thus, despite the demands of her job, she makes some attempt at maintaining work-life balance by engaging in hobbies and taking time away to clear her mind so she can stay mentally and emotionally sharp when focused on her professional obligations.

Grace is also someone who connects with people on an authentic level. She possesses exceptional interpersonal skills; however, in my view the key component that makes her a consummate leader is not her inherent extraversion, but the underlying sincerity in her relationships with others. She has a genuine interest in and curiosity about others, and this concern comes through in her interactions with them. Grace's authenticity also shines in her willingness to speak her mind. She is assertive in voicing her opinions but is always respectful and productive when she does so. As a result, people trust her and want to follow her because they know they are getting the straight story from her, and they believe she has their best interests at heart.

Grace is also optimistic and upbeat. The ability to anticipate the future with a positive outlook not only makes it more pleasant for others to be around her, it also encourages them to develop solutions to problems more effectively. Her ability to enthusiastically paint a picture that inspires others allows her to gain buy-in and build a sense of excitement that encourages others to persist in the face of difficulties or uncertainty.

CHARACTERISTICS OF A CONSUMMATE LEADER

Each of us has the potential to be a consummate leader like Grace. Although no two leaders are going to go about accomplishing goals in exactly the same way, we each have the capacity to inspire others to accomplish great things. Every one of us has the ability to help others grow by encouraging them to stretch beyond what they may have thought possible. And by helping others to perform at their peaks, we can achieve outstanding results for our organizations, whether they are businesses, community groups, or our families.

There is no cookie-cutter approach to managing people. Because we are all different, there is plenty of room to put our own personal stamps on our approaches to leadership. This is why I believe that it is most important to develop the aspects of our character that underlie whatever leadership choices we make, as opposed to merely focusing on specific techniques.

Based on my years of experience dealing with leaders, I have identified seven key characteristics that are found in consummate leaders.

1. SELF-AWARENESS

Socrates' advice to "Know thyself" is critical for any leader (and actually, for anybody who has interactions with other human beings). Without an in-depth understanding of your values, strengths, weaknesses, triggers, and the like, you leave yourself susceptible to blindly reacting to occurrences in your environment. By having the goal of continuously learning about one of the most interesting people on the planet – you! – you can prevent yourself from becoming stagnant and work toward fulfilling your potential.

2. Spirituality

A consummate leader views her career as a calling of sorts and finds a sense of meaning and purpose in her work. Whether or not she is religious, per se, she is inspired to make a contribution to her organization, her colleagues, and the community through her work. This sense of purpose enables her to persist when the going gets tough, and the sense of passion she exudes for her work is motivating to those around her.

3. Self-Management

A consummate leader is skilled at managing himself. He understands his emotional hang-ups and how his thoughts and beliefs can have the potential to trip him up. He focuses on having a positive mindset that allows him to confidently take on challenges. He is willing to take calculated risks, but when setbacks occur, he is able to maintain perspective, learn from the disappointment, and be better equipped the next time a similar challenge arises. In addition to putting energy into his work life, he understands the importance of tending to his life outside of work so he can be a healthy and balanced human being. He engages in hobbies and takes care of his body so he can recharge effectively during his off-time. This enables him to have the energy at work needed to put forth his best effort and achieve the greatest results.

4. POSITIVITY

A consummate leader maintains a positive outlook. She knows that focusing on being happy and grateful not only helps her to feel better, it also creates better organizational outcomes. Although she is not a naïve Pollyanna, she expects the best of people and of situations. She realizes that employees want to follow someone who gives them a sense of hope, and her positive attitude enables her to create the air of excitement required to catalyze people to accomplish great things.

5. AUTHENTICITY

A consummate leader is genuine, open, and comfortable in his own skin. He has his own opinions and is comfortable voicing them respectfully in a way that others are able to hear. Though he does not seek out conflict, he realizes that differences of opinion arise in the workplace and cannot be ignored. He is able to set boundaries and address difficult issues, and in so doing, gains others' respect. He recognizes that to earn his seat at the table, he needs to express his perspectives directly.

6. EFFECTIVE RELATIONSHIP BUILDING

In organizations, work gets done through people. It makes sense that people are most likely to want to work for and be influenced by people with whom they have good relationships, and consummate leaders recognize this truism. While I have heard some people describe relationship building in pejorative terms such as "schmoozing," the reality is that human beings are social creatures. Given the choice between working with someone who is competent and standoffish versus someone who is competent and warm, who wouldn't choose the latter? A consummate leader understands that most people want to have pleasant interactions at work, and by connecting with others to put their audiences in a more positive state of mind, they are able to be more effective.

7. Skillful Coaching and Developing

Consummate leaders are able to get the best out of the people who work for them, and they understand that the only way to do this is by being intentional about employee development. Just as a skillful coach can help a young athlete to capitalize on her gifts and improve the weaker aspects of her game, an adept coach in the business world can assist his employees in broadening their skills and shoring up their weaknesses so they can advance in their careers. In both cases, the team benefits from the individuals' successes.

How to Use This Book

In the chapters that follow, I will be describing each of the characteristics of a consummate leader in greater detail and providing you with tools and exercises to develop each of these qualities in yourself. While this book could potentially be a fairly quick read, and you could learn a good deal by skimming through it, you will not accomplish much in terms of your personal growth by doing so.

Instead, to get the most out of this book, you will need to take your time to reflect on the questions I pose and work through the suggested exercises. Many of my clients find it helpful to maintain a journal in which they can answer questions, make notes on any insights that arise, and keep track of how they are progressing toward their goals. Research shows that self-monitoring (writing things down) increases the odds for success when making personal changes. Therefore, I encourage you to keep a journal, make notes on a tablet, or find some other strategy that works for you to get your thoughts out as you work through the book.

I cannot stress enough the importance of taking your time with this endeavor. Just as researching the proper technique for doing a backflip may provide you with some theoretical knowledge, you can't actually have a hope of becoming the next Gabrielle Douglas without some practice. Likewise, while reading the various exercises that I suggest will make you a more informed individual, actually taking the time to put in the work and try out the activities will be where the rubber meets the road in terms of your development.

Finally, even if you are not yet in a position in which you are leading people, working on these seven areas will be an excellent preparation to ready yourself for the opportunity when it arises. In fact, going through this process may make you a more attractive candidate for promotions. I believe that we all have the potential to be consummate leaders with enough effort and attention, and I encourage you to now take on the challenge to become one!

Leadership is a potent combination of strategy and character. But if you must be without one, be without the strategy.

—NORMAN SCHWARZKOPF

CHAPTER TWO

Self-Awareness

He who knows others is wise.
He who knows himself is enlightened.

—Lao Tzu

Of all the characteristics of the consummate leader, self-awareness is the most important. Quite frankly, I believe it is impossible to be a great leader without it. If you don't have an in-depth understanding of your strengths, how can you possibly leverage them to your best advantage? If you are unaware of the areas on which you need to work, how can you prevent yourself from allowing them to potentially derail you? If you don't know the prospective baggage you could be dragging around, how can you make sure that it doesn't unduly affect your decisions or interactions with others?

The importance of self-awareness is illustrated in the example of Tessa, an executive I once coached who worked in the finance area of a non-profit organization. Her boss, Anne, was hoping that Tessa could become her successor in the future, but she had some significant concerns about a few aspects of her style. On the positive, Tessa was seen as someone who was incredibly dedicated to her job. She had an outstanding work ethic, and she was consistently one of the first people to arrive at the office in the morning and one of the last to leave at the end of the day. She was attentive to detail, knowledgeable about her field, and always willing to go the extra mile to help others. She was logical, practical, and focused on generating the highest quality work product for those around her.

While some of Tessa's responsibilities involved "number-crunching," a lot of her work required her to get things done through people over whom she had no authority. For example, one of her tasks was to put together financial reports for Anne to present to senior executives. This was frequently challenging as it required her to collect information from coworkers, many of whom had no interest in administrative matters and did not see her requests as being a top priority.

Another one of Tessa's responsibilities was to enforce organizational policies. Clearly, this aspect of her role required her to address others' misbehaviors and say "no" a lot of the time, which certainly didn't always ingratiate her with others. Anne perceived Tessa as struggling and asked me to work with her to help her to be more effective.

When I first spoke with Tessa, she was at a loss as to why people tended to be unwilling to comply with her requests for information. For example, when she was in the process of putting together one of her monthly reports, she would reach out to coworkers, most frequently by email, requesting the data she required. She saw herself as the victim who was at their mercy, as they would often ignore her emails or only respond after numerous reminders and reprisals. She found the situation incredibly frustrating since in her view, she was simply doing her best to complete her responsibilities, persisting to get the job done despite obstacles erected by unprofessional colleagues.

Tessa also felt that Anne's concerns about her performance were unfair. While it was true that people frequently gave her a hard time, she still managed to deliver on what was asked of her. Also, she felt Anne didn't understand the stress she was under as a result of dealing with uncooperative coworkers, not to mention caring for her aging mother. Tessa knew that others would "screw her over" if given the opportunity, and her coworkers' behavior clearly proved this belief to be true.

As a starting point in our work together, we conducted a psychological assessment and a 360° survey. The assessment included an interview and some problem-solving and personality testing to provide us with objective data about her psychological makeup, strengths, and opportunities for growth. The 360° survey (a tool used to solicit feedback from Tessa's boss, direct reports, and peers) allowed her coworkers to anonymously report their assessments of her strengths and developmental opportunities as another source of information upon which we could draw.

The strengths that emerged from her assessment were just as we would have expected: Tessa's data showed that she was hardworking, responsive, disciplined, organized, reliable, and results oriented. However, many of the areas for development came as a surprise to Tessa. The results of the assessment and the feedback suggested that she could be rigid and unwilling to entertain others' perspectives. She had unrealistic expectations of others and could actually be critical or sarcastic in her interactions with them. Because she was shy and private, she didn't focus on building relationships with others; in fact, she made a concerted effort to compartmentalize her work life from her personal life. And, while her results orientation could be a strength, the flip side of it was that she quickly became impatient when others weren't responding to her requests at her desired rate.

It became clear that coworkers did not want to go out of their way to help Tessa when she made requests of them because their interactions with her were usually unpleasant. Because she only interacted with her colleagues when she wanted something from them, they never had the opportunity to get to know her as a whole person; instead, they knew her as "that person in finance" who was always making requests of them, sometimes brusquely. They further saw her as someone who was never willing to listen to their side of the story; rather, she was always quick to deny their requests without explanation or discussion, sometimes with a cutting remark and a smirk thrown in for good measure.

Before receiving the feedback, Tessa could not think of anything she could do differently to encourage people to be more willing to help her. In her opinion, the issue was her coworkers' irresponsibility, as they were simply not responding to her appeals for assistance. In her view, if the shoe had been on the other foot and someone had sent her an email asking for information, she would respond to it in a timely manner, since "that is what a responsible worker does!" She genuinely could not fathom any alternative explanations for the struggles she was having, aside from the conclusion she had reached that her coworkers were ne'er-do-wells.

After receiving the feedback, she still maintained that none of her liabilities *should* have affected her coworkers' willingness to cooperate with her, since providing her with information was in the best interest of the organization. However, with a greater awareness of how she was coming across, she was at least able to entertain the idea that she might be contributing to the difficulty she was having, and that by changing her behavior, she may achieve better results.

TRUCKING ALONG

Tessa's case is a clear example of how limited self-understanding can reduce one's effectiveness. Not only was she unaware of the negative impact she was having on others, she was so focused on blaming others that she was unwilling to even consider that her approach might play a role in their responses to her. In other words, by continually looking outward instead of inward, she wasn't following the prudent advice from Luke 6:42: "How can you say to your brother, 'Brother, let me take the speck out of your eye,' when you yourself fail to see the plank in your own eye? You hypocrite, first take the plank out of your eye, and then you will see clearly to remove the speck from your brother's eye."

One of my wittier clients has a running joke with his colleagues that I once told him he has a "blind spot the size of a trucker." While I would never say such a thing to anyone (or at least not to his face), his notion is a useful metaphor. Think of it: a trucker with a massive blind spot still has a pretty good likelihood of being able to get to his desired destination. However, on the way there, he may unintentionally disturb those around him by cutting them off, creating unpleasant driving conditions, and putting them on edge. In the worst case scenario, he could cause an accident that makes accomplishing his goal of completing a delivery impossible.

On the other hand, a trucker who has all her mirrors positioned to avoid blind spots is able to make her delivery effectively, taking the most direct route without causing difficulty for the other drivers with whom she shares the road. Clearly, consummate leaders want to be the second sort of trucker, who have no blind spots and can maneuver efficiently.

Quite simply, people who are self-aware interact more effectively with others than those who are not. They know how they are likely to be coming across, and they take steps to ensure they monitor themselves to increase their chances of being perceived as intended. They can sense when they are getting upset or defensive and make sure they are managing their emotions so they don't create issues in their relationships with others. They are aware of the sides of themselves that can prevent them from working at their peaks, whether it is a tendency to be disorganized, a potential to come across as aloof, or a fear of taking risks, for example. They actively work to make sure they are taking advantage of their strengths, and they consistently focus on minimizing and/or developing the areas that need work. In this way, they fulfill their potential in the workplace.

HOW TO BECOME MORE SELF-AWARE

> *Who in the world am I? Ah, that's the great puzzle.*
> —Lewis Carroll, *Alice in Wonderland*

The task of becoming more self-aware is an ongoing process that requires a spirit of curiosity and a willingness to learn. Your goal in this respect is to develop a balanced, well-rounded view of yourself. All of us have strengths and areas in need of work, and your task in increasing your level of self-awareness is to learn about all sides of yourself, without judgment. As the rabbi and author Joshua Liebman asserted: "Self-understanding rather than self-condemnation is the way to inner peace and mature conscience."

If you can take the perspective of viewing life as a journey during which you will always have opportunities to gain deeper insights into yourself and find new areas in which to develop, you will be in the right frame of mind to self-reflect and grow. While some people view the need for personal development as suggesting they have some sort of deficiency, a healthier view is to think of yourself as always being able to be fine-tuned and developed. So, with that in mind, let's begin to explore a number of strategies you can use to increase your level of self-awareness.

1. WRITE DOWN YOUR STRENGTHS AND WEAKNESSES

A good starting point for self-discovery is to take stock of your strengths and developmental opportunities.[1] Your aim is to make an exhaustive list of all the areas in which you are strong, and all the areas on which you need to work. In addition to listing *behaviors* at which you are good (e.g., meeting deadlines, making sales, doing math), list adjectives to describe yourself in terms of your *personality characteristics* (e.g., compassionate, outgoing, hardworking). Use this same process when listing your developmental opportunities.

For example, some behaviors in need of work may include public speaking, listening, or delegating, while some personality characteristics you address may be shyness, impatience, or low assertiveness. Try to be as specific as possible as you create your list. So, instead of listing "being a great leader" as a strength, think about the qualities you possess that make you a strong leader. Ask yourself, for example:

- *Am I someone who is visionary and can rally the troops to follow me?*
- *Am I someone who is compassionate and able to create a comfortable environment in which others can stretch themselves and take risks?*
- *Am I knowledgeable in my area of expertise and able to teach people?*

As you self-reflect, think about yourself in both your personal and professional pursuits. For example, I have seen some individuals who are highly involved leaders in their community organizations but have not had the opportunity to display these skills in the workplace. Conversely, I have interacted with some highly organized and driven stay-at-home mothers who are adept leaders in their households or in their children's activities. Even if you have not yet been able to demonstrate your leadership at work, it doesn't mean it is not a strength for you; perhaps you simply need to be intentional with respect to figuring out how to show this quality to others in your organization.

While some people have an easy time determining their strengths and developmental opportunities, others can have some difficulty with this exercise. For example, I have come across clients who are so self-critical that they struggle to think of any positive qualities they may possess. If this is you, I insist you set a goal of coming up with *at least* 10 positive qualities – even if you are having a hard time – while doing this exercise. *Everyone* has strengths. Think about successes you have had in your life and reflect on your qualities that contributed to them. What are you proudest of? Where are you most effective? If, after putting in a good deal of effort, you find you are still having difficulty coming up with your strengths, refer to the Appendix for some ideas. Make sure, though, to give it your best effort first or you will deprive yourself of this useful exercise in introspection and self-discovery.

In contrast to the overly self-critical, I have also worked with individuals who have difficulty recognizing their developmental opportunities. If this is you, take this exercise seriously, as I can almost guarantee you have a blind spot (since none of us is perfect). Think about times when situations haven't gone as planned. How may you have contributed to these events? Also consider that sometimes our strengths, when taken to extremes, can become developmental opportunities.

For example, while being an enthusiastic talker is a strength, it can become a liability if others have difficulty getting a word in edgewise. Likewise, although being thoughtful while making decisions is an asset, it can work against you if you consistently take so long to take action that you miss out on opportunities.

Do you have any strengths that you need to monitor to ensure they don't become liabilities for you? Look through the strengths list in the Appendix and consider whether your lack of a given strength – or an overplayed one – can work against you in some areas.

Make it a habit to pay attention, self-reflect, and internalize others' feedback so you can continue to add or remove items from your list over time.

2. Take Personality Measures

Another effective way to improve your level of self-insight is to take objective personality measures. If you are able to do so, it can be valuable to meet with a psychologist who is adept at career counseling or executive coaching, as he can conduct a psychological assessment that will provide you with greater self-understanding. While the specific instruments used in an assessment will vary, they may include cognitive tests, personality instruments, and/or an interview. If you are unable to meet with a psychologist, I recommend searching online for personality instruments. You will not have access to many of the ones a psychologist is able to use (as many require education and training to interpret ethically and effectively), but it can still be a helpful means of learning more about yourself.

Once you have received the output from the instruments, be sure to add to your list of strengths and developmental opportunities. As you review the data you receive from a computerized assessment, it is normal if you feel like there are certain things that may not apply to you – human beings are complex, and there is only so much a computer-generated report based on general population norms can explain. For now, however, write down the characteristics or behaviors about which you are uncertain, and put a question mark beside them on your list. As you pay closer attention to yourself and your behaviors in your daily life, try to monitor if these characteristics about which you were uncertain actually *are* true for you.

3. SEEK FEEDBACK

Another important means of increasing self-awareness is to ask others for feedback. By its very definition, if you have a blind spot, the only way to become aware of it is for others to tell you about it. I recommend seeking feedback from as many people as you possibly can, and make it an ongoing practice. In addition to being a great way to learn about yourself and how you are perceived, it can be a valuable means of building relationships.

I have found that a lot of us have a love-hate relationship with feedback. Most of us love getting positive recognition for things we do well; after all, who doesn't love a good compliment? I've even known some people who enjoyed it so much they would toot their own horn before I had the opportunity!

On the other hand, a lot of us find constructive criticism a whole lot less palatable. Even for those of us who recognize the benefits of it on a theoretical level, it can still cause a bit of an emotional sting when we actually hear it. But, if you think about it, feedback (even of the negative variety) is a gift. It means that someone cares enough to give you guidance to help you improve or to make a better impression on others.

For example, if you were unknowingly walking around with spinach in your teeth (a great example of a blind spot), wouldn't you want to know about it? Similarly, wouldn't you want to know if everyone in the office thinks you come across as arrogant? Feedback is empowering, as it provides you with additional information and greater self-awareness. Even if you disagree with some feedback you receive, at the very least it will give you greater insight into how others may perceive you.

While most people are happy to tell others about their strengths, a lot of us are uncomfortable telling them about areas upon which they can work. How many of us have been told, "If you can't say anything nice, don't say anything at all"? Since many of us experience a negative emotional reaction in response to constructive criticism, we are reluctant to take the risk to give others negative feedback for fear that we may hurt their feelings. However, if you understand how difficult it can be for others to give you feedback, you will realize how important it is for you to make it as easy for them as possible.

To receive the highest quality feedback, therefore, it is your job to make it a pleasant experience for both parties.

To ensure a productive experience on your end, it is critical to prepare yourself appropriately before asking for feedback by anticipating the sorts of reactions you may have. The acronym "SARA" is used to describe the four types of responses you are likely to experience when receiving negative feedback.

First, you may be *surprised*. Like Tessa, if you are getting feedback you have never heard before, you are likely to be a little shocked or unsettled in response to it. Second, you may become *angry*. I can think of several occasions in which I have received unsolicited feedback (usually from a significant other), during which I became annoyed and felt a need to provide him or her with some unsolicited feedback of my own! (It doesn't take a psychologist to predict that engaging in that sort of behavior probably isn't going to accomplish the goal of making the feedback experience a pleasant one!) Third, you may *rationalize*. This involves explaining away the feedback and minimizing its importance. Finally, you can hopefully get to the point at which you *accept* the feedback.

By expecting certain internal responses, you can put yourself in a better position to monitor your reactions so that you don't ruin all chances of ever getting feedback again. In fact, when someone is providing you with feedback, stay calm (breathe deeply if you need to, to keep your mind and body relaxed) and control your nonverbal reactions (now is not the time to roll your eyes or look incredulous, even if you are shocked). Ask questions in the habit of striving to understand what the other person is saying, without being defensive. When you are receiving feedback, do not argue or explain yourself. Simply allow the person you are speaking with to explain himself, then say "thank you."

It can also be helpful to provide others with context when you are asking for feedback. For example, you may tell a coworker that you are working on your professional development, and you have picked her to give you her perspective because she is someone you trust and whose opinion you value. Depending on the person, she may need some time to think about what she would like to say. As such, it's usually helpful to give her a heads up about the sorts of questions you will be asking.

If you are a senior person asking for feedback from someone who is at a lower level within the organization, it will be particularly important to make sure you take the time to put the other person at ease. If, in response to your request for feedback, he responds that you have nothing to work on, gently encourage him to really think about it, letting him know that he can sincerely help you by providing you with ideas about areas for growth. Asking people who report to you for feedback is also an excellent way of modeling the sort of behavior that will enable them to develop more quickly. So, make sure you model an openness to hearing about ways in which you can improve.

Some sample questions you may ask include:

- What do you think I'm good at? What are my strengths?
- What do you think I need to work on to be more effective and achieve my maximum potential?
- What sorts of things should I stop doing? Why?
- What should I continue doing? Why?
- What would you like me to do more of? Why?
- What is my greatest contribution to the organization?
- How do I most detract from the organization?

If you happened to have taken any personality instruments and had some areas that came up about which you were uncertain, you may want to ask others for feedback about them, as well as address to possible blind spots. A question you may ask to get at this would be, "Have you noticed any times when I do *behavior X*?"

Don't forget that it is critical to respond positively when you are receiving feedback. Watch out for your reactions! Providing feedback is a skill (one that we will talk about later in this book), and so try to be forgiving if others' attempts to do so are somewhat clunky. If they seem to be sugarcoating it, try to guide them to be more direct (without sounding like you are engaging in an inquisition).

Similarly, if the feedback is coming across more abruptly than you may have liked, listen to the content of what they are presenting, as opposed to the way in which they are saying it. Try to separate yourself from the emotions of the situation so you can gain the most benefit from the information with which you are presented. Make sure to do this even when asking for feedback from those who are close to you. Remember, the purpose of this exercise is to help you grow, not to get even with others. Also, if you make giving feedback a painful experience for the other person, you will likely never receive it from her again!

Finally, if you have the resources, a 360° or multi-rater survey can be a helpful means of receiving feedback. As noted previously, a 360° survey is an instrument designed to allow others to provide you with anonymous feedback, through a series of questions that tap into particular work-related behaviors on a numerical scale. As a result, you can get a sense of how others rate you in a variety of areas, determining your relative strengths and developmental opportunities based on the numbers. If you decide to use a 360° survey, I would encourage you to follow up to ask some of the people who rated you for in-person feedback. Not only will it provide you with a richer understanding of their perspectives, it can also be helpful for deepening relationships.

Look for themes in the feedback you receive and add them to your list of strengths and developmental opportunities, which by this point, should be pretty well rounded.

GOING DEEPER

> *Until we see what we are,*
> *we cannot take steps to become what we should be.*
> —Charlotte P. Gilman

The strategies I listed in the previous section are an excellent way to get started with respect to increasing your level of self-awareness. However, in my view, they are only a start. This next step is an opportunity for you to engage in deeper self-examination so you can have an even greater understanding of yourself.

Very often in business, people like to limit their self-exploration to thinking about themselves purely in the work setting. I believe this is a mistake. As I noted in the introduction, when I engaged in development that was entirely focused on my personal life, it inadvertently had a positive impact at work. Similarly, I am sure we have all come across people whose difficulties in their personal lives bleed over into their work lives, despite concerted attempts to keep their personal and professional lives separate. This is why a holistic approach to leadership development is so important – we are whole people and our whole selves show up wherever we go.

Therefore, this next step will require you to take a good, hard look at yourself. I will be encouraging you to reflect on your developmental history, family background, world views, and the like. For many of you, it may be a difficult exercise, as you will be faced with questions about which you may have never put much thought. That's okay – take it as a sign that this is an area in which you can learn a lot!

I would encourage you not to rush through this portion of the book. Even if you struggle to answer the questions initially, tuck them away in your mind or make a note in your journal. Across time, with additional reflection, you may come up with valuable new insights a few days, a few months, or even a few years from now.

TELL ME ABOUT YOUR CHILDHOOD ...

We are going to start with having you consider your family history. I know, I know, some of you may be rolling your eyes right now as you think about the stereotype of the psychologist asking you to lie back on the couch and talk about your mother. Rest assured, however, that in this day and age, most psychologists actually allow you to sit up in a vertical position! Seriously, though, for those of you who are uncomfortable with this and are tempted to skip ahead, bear with me for a minute and consider my rationale.

First, even if you don't enjoy thinking about topics like this, it is hard to deny that your family experiences had a measurable impact on shaping you. So if you truly want to understand yourself, this is something you need to think about. Second, just to put your mind at ease, this is not going to turn into an assignment of blaming mommy and daddy. It is my opinion that even people who are less-than-optimal parents tend to be doing the best they can do, given their background, issues, and knowledge at any given time. So, I am asking you to reflect on these topics to gain an objective understanding of *yourself*, as opposed to pointing fingers.

Third, I am solution focused, and as a result, I don't believe you necessarily need to engage in years of analysis and psychotherapy to unlearn various behaviors. However, if you are unaware of them and how they came to be, it is much more difficult to address them. This exercise is designed to give you a bit more insight into where certain tendencies originated.

Finally, I can honestly say that while I have worked with individuals who have developed significantly as a result of engaging in the sorts of exercises I suggested earlier in this chapter, those who have made the greatest gains are the ones who have been willing to work harder and grapple with deeper issues, such as the ones on which we are going to now focus.

Going deeper by answering the questions on the next several pages should not be an exercise that you gloss over quickly. If you do it properly, it should be a process that takes you some time to complete. Thus, even after taking your first stab at answering the questions, it is likely that you will continue to gain insights that will further deepen your self-understanding across time.

To start, I want you to think back to your family of origin (the people around whom you grew up) and answer the following questions (I suggest you write down your responses in a journal).

1. Who comprised your family? Who were the significant people in your life when you were growing up?

2. How would you describe your mother? What were her positive qualities? What were her not-so-positive qualities? How are you most like her? How are you most different from her? How did she affect your development? What lessons (good and bad) did you learn from her?

3. How would you describe your father? What were his positive qualities? What were his not-so-positive qualities? How are you most like him? How are you most different from him? How did he affect your development? What lessons (good and bad) did you learn from him?

As you think about the impact your parents had on your development, try to be as balanced as possible. For example, some people may report that their father taught them integrity, honesty, and how to treat others. Some may report that because their father wasn't around much, he didn't have an impact on them. In this case, you might consider what effect his *absence* had on you. Did it teach you to be more independent? Did it cause you to be wary of people?

Also, think about behaviors your parents modeled for you. Some people indicate that they learned hard work and dedication through watching a parent who was committed to providing for the family. In other cases, people report that their parent showed them what not to do, and as a result, they decided to behave differently. Alternately, we may at times pick up unwanted habits from our parents.

Remember, there is no perfect parent, and even wonderful parents sometimes unintentionally shape their kids in not-so-perfect ways. For example, a parent may have taught you to be competitive and strive for perfection. However, did this have a flip side of making you fear failure and be reluctant to take risks?

Remember, this exercise is not about placing blame; rather, it is about helping you to fully understand yourself on a deep level. Also, keep in mind that the same experience can affect two people in different ways. The key of this exercise is to consider how it affected *you*.

4. Did you have any other significant parental figures, such as grandparents or stepparents? What were their positive qualities? What were their not-so-positive qualities? How are you most like them? How are you most different from them? How did they affect your development? What lessons (good and bad) did you learn from them?

5. Do you have siblings? Are they older or younger than you? How did you interact with them? What were each of your psychological roles in the family?

6. What was it like growing up in your home? How close was your family? How did they communicate with one another?

7. What were your relationships like with peers? How were you viewed by classmates? How did that shape you?

8. Were there any other significant people who affected you in your childhood (e.g., coaches, teachers, religious figures)? How did they influence you?

9. What were your greatest challenges in childhood? What were your greatest triumphs? How did these shape you?

10. Were there any significant events that occurred as you were growing up? For example, did your parents get divorced? Did you move? Did you deal with any deaths? Did you experience successes in hobbies or extracurricular activities? How did these shape your outlook?

As you reflect on these various questions, you may be having some "aha" moments or connecting some dots that give you greater insight into why you do some of the things you do, or why you look at things a certain way. Also, as you compare yourself to other people, it may give you some additional ideas about strengths you possess and developmental opportunities on which you can work. Having this knowledge can better inform your ability to work through issues that may affect you as a leader.

Now, move ahead to your current situation:

11. Do you have a significant other? What was it about this person that attracted you? How does he or she complement you? How would he or she describe you in terms of your strengths and developmental opportunities?

12. Do you have children? How are they most like you? What have you learned about yourself through the parenting process?

13. Do you have any failed long-term relationships? What did you learn from these experiences? How did you contribute to the outcome of the relationship? Does that experience affect your current interactions with others?

Again, each of these questions is designed to help you to look at yourself objectively, to have a greater understanding of yourself, and to note any patterns that may cause issues for you.

Let's say, for example, that a marriage ended because your spouse cheated on you. Obviously that person violated a boundary in the relationship. However, is there anything you can learn about yourself as a result of having gone through that experience? For example:

- Did you ignore gut instincts?
- Has the experience affected your ability to trust and connect with others?
- Did your perfectionism and critical attitude contribute to making your partner feel unwanted?

The key here is not to place blame, but to learn about yourself in a compassionate way. Even if you make every attempt to compartmentalize your work self from your home self, it is likely that your core characteristics show themselves in both arenas. Self-knowledge is power.

Let's now focus on some more global questions:

14. How do you view people? Do you think they are inherently good? Do you believe you have to be on guard around them? Where did you get those ideas from?

15. Were there any significant events that shaped you during your adulthood? How did they affect you? For example:

- Did you have a boss or mentor who influenced your outlook?
- Did you go through a divorce?
- Did you have any health issues?
- Did you have any accomplishments that shaped your view of yourself?
- Did you have any major disappointments that influenced you?

16. What drives you?
17. What are you afraid of? Why?
18. How are you most likely to be misperceived by other people? How do you contribute to these misunderstandings?
19. What are you like under stress? What triggers cause you to have an undesirable response?
20. What aspects of yourself would you change if you could?

At this point, you should have a lot of information on which to reflect. To help you to pull it together coherently, answer the following questions:

1. What insights have I gained that help me better understand how I deal with people?
2. What insights have I gained that help me better understand how I approach my work?
3. What are the best parts of my personality? What strengths have I developed as a result of my varied experiences?
4. What developmental opportunities need to be addressed to allow me to maximize my potential?

Use your journal to keep track of the various insights you will continue to learn about yourself. When one of the behaviors that is problematic for you arises, notice what might be contributing to it. Are you able to identify any triggers?

When you are experiencing a day during which you are at your best, take note of what influences that as well. As you notice patterns, you will put yourself in a much better position to manage your behaviors and reactions. That is what being a consummate leader is all about.

As you continue through the book, you will be doing a lot more self-examination before pulling it all together to create a plan of attack for your professional development. However, even at this point, you may find that pondering these questions has given you some valuable insights that can guide your efforts to grow. Read on for a brief example of how delving into your history can increase your self-awareness and ability to be your best.

Case Study

Evan was a talented consultant who was recognized in his firm as someone who was creative, articulate, intelligent, and skilled at developing solutions. In his job, there were two major outcomes for which he was responsible. The first was helping clients by providing them with wise counsel to assist them in making decisions. He excelled in this aspect of his role – he was a responsive professional who genuinely enjoyed assisting others and loved the challenge of solving a puzzle.

The second aspect of work, however, which was to sell to clients and bring in new business, was more difficult for him. Despite the fact that he managed his time effectively in other areas, he consistently procrastinated when it came to sales and marketing activities. He would tell himself he didn't have the time to reach out to potential clients or that selling was actually "sleazy," and as such, he needed to devote himself to the "more honorable" work of actually helping people. While his rationalizations helped him to feel fine about focusing on the work with which he was more comfortable, he knew deep down that his excuses also limited his progress and the level of recognition he was able to attain within his company.

After some self-reflection, Evan came to realize that some of the experiences of his youth had shaped his beliefs and expectations. He had been born to a young unwed mother. His biological father was an irresponsible and somewhat self-absorbed man who relied on others to keep him financially afloat. Despite Evan's desires, he was unable to develop a close relationship with his father. In fact, he remembered several occasions during which he would wait in vain for his father to visit, as promised, only to end up feeling disappointed, wondering what he had done wrong to make his father not want to see him. Eventually, he "hardened" himself and developed a sense of apathy about that relationship.

Evan's mother eventually married, and he had two much younger half-siblings. While his stepfather was a positive influence in his life, he (perhaps unwittingly) favored his biological children. While they were cute and charming preschoolers who could seemingly do no wrong, Evan was an awkward adolescent who was held to different standards. As a result, Evan frequently felt like an outsider at home. The one area in which Evan excelled, however, was academics. He had always been one of the top students in his class, and in addition to winning awards at school, he always received praise for his academic ability from his mother and stepfather, who would describe him as the "family brain." Despite his insecurities in some areas, he always had a strong sense of self-assurance about his intellect based on his parents' accolades and his stellar report cards.

As a result of contemplating these aspects of his childhood, Evan was better able to understand his current work situation. He realized that he excelled in the technical areas of his job that required him to engage his intellect. This was an area about which he felt confident and competent, and his work reflected that. Sales, however, brought up some uncomfortable feelings for him. Inherent in sales is the possibility of rejection; he could put forth his best effort and still have someone decide that she didn't want to work with him. Evan also had the insight that in his personal life, he tended to avoid situations in which he might experience feelings of rejection.

Just as he had developed a sense of apathy about his father, he had become an eternal bachelor who hadn't found a suitable woman to commit to because he "just wasn't quite ready and couldn't find the right woman." He recognized that he had actually developed an expectation that he was going to be rejected when selling to others, whether personally or professionally. Further, he identified his procrastination and rationalizations related to sales as a form of self-protection that prevented him from "putting himself out there" and potentially getting hurt or rejected. This understanding was the first step in being able to address his issues related to sales.

It takes courage ... to endure the sharp pains of self-discovery rather than choose to take the dull pain of unconsciousness that would last the rest of our lives.

—MARIANNE WILLIAMSON

CHAPTER THREE

SPIRITUALITY

It isn't until you come to a spiritual understanding of who you are - not necessarily a religious feeling, but deep down, the spirit within - that you can begin to take control.

—OPRAH WINFREY

I almost didn't include this chapter. As one senior banking executive who was a devout Christian said to me, "My faith is deeply important to me, but I can't really talk about it at work."

I'm sensitive to the fact that people can be reticent to talk about faith in the workplace. After all, spirituality is a deeply personal topic, and it's one about which people have some very strong convictions. I have witnessed conversations in which the topic of faith created a sense of divisiveness instead of closeness in a group because individuals were unwilling to respect their colleague's right to have different beliefs. I have seen leaders abuse religion in the workplace to the extent that their employees felt they were working under some sort of patriarchy in which only one view of the world was deemed to be an acceptable one. I have observed people who were of a religion that was non-dominant in the U.S., such as Buddhism or Islam, who carefully kept their religious affiliations secret for fear they would be ostracized by non-tolerant others.

I point these areas out to underscore that I get it. Religion is a touchy topic, and one that, like politics, we have been taught is generally prudent to avoid discussing in mixed company. In some of the interviews I have conducted as a corporate psychologist, I have seen people tentatively mention the topic of their faith as if they were putting it out there, like a test balloon, to see how I would respond. When I openly and non-judgmentally engaged them on the topic, they became visibly more relaxed, as if some sort of burden had been lifted off them, causing them to feel at liberty to talk about a central part of their identity that shaped every aspect of their daily lives.

According to a recent Gallup survey, Americans' confidence in organized religion is at an all-time low of 44% since 1973 (when they started collecting data on the topic).[2] At the same time, however, 92% of Americans report that they believe in God.[3]

Given that my purpose in writing this book is to put forth a holistic guide to leadership that goes deeper than other books typically do, it would be remiss of me to avoid a topic that is relevant to the vast majority of the population simply because it may make some people uncomfortable. Also, based on my experience coaching leaders, I have seen how accessing one's spirituality can enhance one's leadership skills and general effectiveness in the workplace.

Spirituality is something that you don't necessarily need to talk about at work, but if you don't reflect on it for yourself, you are probably missing out on an important opportunity. So, because it is my intention to give you the tools I believe are most important to becoming a consummate leader, I have decided to include this chapter.

WHAT IS SPIRITUALITY?

While the two concepts are intertwined for many people, for the purpose of this chapter, I am drawing a distinction between spirituality and religion. Whereas religion is defined by Webster's New Universal Unabridged Dictionary as "any specific system of belief, worship, conduct, etc., often involving a code of ethics and a philosophy ..." spirituality is defined as "the quality or state of being spiritual" or "sensitivity or attachment to religious values." Thus, religiosity is associated with an organized institution having a prescribed set of practices and beliefs, whereas spirituality is defined more broadly as having spiritual values (although they may or may not be strictly associated with a specific organization or religion, per se). As opposed to espousing any particular religious ideology, my focus in this chapter is on spirituality.

Peterson and Seligman[4] argued that spirituality is universal: "Although the specific content of spiritual beliefs varies, all cultures have a concept of an ultimate, transcendent, sacred, and divine force." At the core, therefore, spirituality is a belief in something greater than oneself. Along with this is often the idea that we are here for a reason, that we have a purpose, and by living in accordance with that purpose, we can live fuller, happier, more productive lives. Determining one's purpose and ensuring he or she is living in accordance with it, is a lifelong pursuit for many people. Having an attitude of curiosity, as is required for developing self-awareness (as covered in the previous chapter), also forms the foundation for doing effective spiritual exploration.

To begin to explore how your spirituality informs your life and work, reflect on the following questions:

1. What (if any) spiritual practice did I have in my formative years? How did that shape me?
2. What are my views about religion? What feelings come up for me when I think about it?
3. What are my views about spirituality? What feelings come up for me when I think about it?
4. How central is spirituality in my daily life?
5. How do my views about spirituality affect me at work (if at all)?
6. How do my views about spirituality affect how I interact with others (if at all)?

The above questions provide a good starting point for examining your own views about spirituality and religion. As you might expect, I have worked with many people who have had negative experiences with religion and spirituality, and as such, have strong emotions evoked when the topic is discussed. If you are someone for whom religion brings up negative connotations, I still encourage you to continue reading this chapter. I promise, this chapter is not designed to proselytize or to convert you to a certain set of beliefs. Instead, it is designed to encourage you to think about some deep existential questions.

At the very least, contemplating these issues can be another opportunity for you to self-reflect and deepen your level of self-awareness in understanding how your negative views of religion and spirituality may affect you. At the very best, tackling some of the issues in this chapter may cause you to shift some of your perceptions, find a greater sense of meaning in your life and work, and develop a deeper sense of contentment and motivation in your career.

WHAT'S IT ALL FOR ANYHOW?

> *Your purpose in life is to find your purpose and give your whole heart and soul to it.*
> —Gautama Buddha

"Why am I here?"

It is a rare person who has never pondered this question. Exploring the existential issue of determining one's reason for existence is one of the most important exercises in one's life. Many would argue that having a sense of purpose is critical to imbuing life with a sense of meaning and direction; yet, in the hustle and bustle of our daily existence, many of us ignore the call of this significant question.

It is not uncommon in my work with leaders to come across individuals who feel as though they are running on a treadmill in their careers. They are accomplishing all the goals that have been set for them, earning their potential bonuses and salary increases, getting invited to take part in highly visible and prestigious projects, and receiving all the requisite recognition associated with these accomplishments, yet they are unfulfilled by it all. In many cases, their high achievement is rewarded not only with positive reinforcement, but also with higher expectations for success. They are chasing the accolades and money as an end in itself, and finding that despite living a life of comfort (or often, luxury), they still feel a niggling void in their lives.

Without a sense of purpose directing our actions, it is all too easy to mindlessly engage in our work and get caught up in doing for the sake of doing, without experiencing any sense of fulfillment in the process. Without a "North Star" guiding us, we can become ensconced in the trees and lose sense of the forest of our lives. In this scenario, we may consistently have the feeling that our lives would be better if only we had different jobs or responsibilities, yet feel too stuck to do anything about taking action to change things. Why? Because we don't have the slightest clue what else we should be doing.

A sense of purpose provides us with an overarching view of why we are here. It can provide us with motivation when our work piles up or when we are dealing with a difficult situation or person. The feeling that our work is in service to some larger goal can help us to "dig deeper" and persist when the going gets hard. Even when things are going well, having a purpose can provide us with inspiration and passion.

Having a deep feeling of knowing what you are here to do creates a sense of energy, excitement, and direction. Instead of viewing professional life and personal life as two separate entities, people who have a sense of purpose view their work as an extension of who they really are, perhaps even a ministry of sorts, and a means of positively affecting the world.

In fact, there has been research that suggests that when you perceive your job as a "calling," or something about which you are passionate that is fulfilling in its own right, you experience greater job satisfaction than if you simply perceive your work as a "job" or something you do solely to get paid.[5] Further, with a calling mentality, you are likely to have better job performance because you are more committed to putting in the time and energy to be successful. Given that we spend one-third of our lives at work, it is not surprising that seeing your work as a calling generalizes to other aspects of your existence, such as greater life satisfaction and better health.

So how do you find more fulfilling work? We have all heard instances of people who "discovered their purpose," quit their jobs, and totally revamped their lives. We have heard about the woman who left her demanding law career to become a poet. Or the man who realized that accounting wasn't for him, and instead opened a bakery. For many, it may be tempting to view the grass as being greener on the other side of the fence. "If only I had a different job, my life would be better," I have heard some clients say. Still others have said, "Having a sense of purpose is for other people. I have a mortgage and private school fees to pay. I can't run off and "Eat, Pray, Love" my way through far-flung locales!"

While changing careers may be the path to finding purpose in some cases, in many instances, living with a sense of purpose can be a matter of simply making a mental shift.

For example, while many people may view the job of a hospital cleaner as drudgery, in one study, Wrzesniewski and Dutton found that one-third of the people in this role experienced it as a calling.[6] They saw their role from a big picture perspective – as contributing to the health of patients and the functioning of the hospital. Thus, they engaged more with the people around them and went out of their way to make the patients' stays as comfortable as possible. They took pride in attending to the little details that created a beautiful environment. Their colleagues who saw their role merely as a job, however, perceived their position as boring and meaningless. It was the same position, but the sense of purpose that the former group found in their job created a much more pleasant work experience that enabled them to make a greater contribution.

A wonderful illustration of the power of having a purpose is the story of Nelson Mandela, who was imprisoned for 27 years until finally being released in his early 70s. It would be understandable if he had emerged from prison beaten down and bitter. Instead, because of his deep commitment to bettering the lives of others, his purpose upheld his spirits while confined. Because he wanted to positively affect others, during his time in prison, he maintained his desire to see the humanity in everyone, even his jailers. He purposefully looked to find the goodness in each person, refusing to believe that anyone is all bad.

In one account, when he was asked how he survived all that time incarcerated, he responded that he spent the time improving his leadership skills so he could be more effective once he was released. He educated himself to become a better leader, even learning Afrikaans (the language of white South Africans) in the process, in case it should come in handy in the next chapter of his life. With an intense sense of direction, he was able to persist through appalling circumstances and come out a better person with his ultimate goals still intact. His sense of purpose in prison allowed him to focus on the work that was instrumental in his achievement of becoming South Africa's first black president. The degree of resolve and personal strength he showed in the face of adversity is certainly a lesson for all of us.

WHAT'S MY MOTIVATION?

A close cousin to the concept of purpose is the idea of finding meaning in your work. While I see the quest for purpose as determining the big-picture reason for why you exist and what you are meant to do, I conceptualize finding meaning as a process of figuring out what is fulfilling to you in the moment, how it aligns with your values, and what you can learn from your experiences.

While purpose may be something that is perceived as being derived from the outside (for example, those who believe in a higher power might also believe that each of us has been created for a unique purpose), finding meaning in a situation is a more personal endeavor that comes from within.

According to the existential psychologists, the task of finding meaning in our daily activities is one of our key responsibilities as human beings. As Viktor Frankl, a concentration camp survivor and prominent psychiatrist stated:

> Man's search for meaning is the primary motivation in his life ... This meaning is unique and specific in that it must and can be fulfilled by him alone; only then does it achieve a significance which will satisfy his own *will* to meaning.[7]

It may sound simplistic, but the best process by which to find meaning is to consistently look for it. As is the case with finding purpose, it requires one to step back from a day-to-day perspective and look through a longer-term lens. In any given instance, asking yourself what you can learn from a situation is an excellent strategy for creating a sense of meaning.

For example, one of my clients, Keith, was the president of a small business. The challenges of the economic environment and changing patterns in his industry were causing his once profitable facility to lose money. He and his team had attempted all of the strategies that had worked for them in the past, including cutting expenses as much as they possibly could, to no avail. He was feeling paralyzed as a result of all the obstacles he was facing.

Although Keith tried to put on a brave face as he went about his work, the truth was he was feeling beaten down, and the people around him could tell. Research tells us that the leader's mood has an inordinate amount of influence over the tone of the organization.[8] Keith's case was no exception, and his people, who were looking to him to determine how they should feel about the situation, were starting to feel defeated as well.

Luckily, he had enough self-awareness to recognize how his outlook was affecting those around him. So, as a man of deep faith, he began to self-reflect in an effort to find meaning in his state of affairs. After much introspection, he determined that the challenges he was facing provided him with the opportunity to strengthen his leadership skills. While it had been easy to lead when things were going well, he acknowledged that the mark of an exceptional leader was to continue to inspire through hard times.

By bolstering his resilience and deepening his resolve, he knew he could lead his people through this difficult time. Even if things did not work out as they all had hoped, he and his leadership team could rest assured that they had summoned all of their resources to put in their best possible effort. He knew the valuable lessons this experience taught him would benefit him in this role and beyond.

So how exactly do you go about finding a sense of meaning in your life and work? As was the case in the past two chapters about increasing your level of self-awareness, it comes down to engaging in self-reflection. Work your way through the following questions to begin the process of exploring the issues of purpose and meaning in your career.

1. When you were a child or teenager, what sort of dreams did you have for yourself in terms of your career? What did you hope to be doing? Why? What about that was appealing to you?
2. Thinking on a very broad level, why do you think you are here on earth? What are you meant to do? What unique gifts are you able to contribute?

3. Think of times during your career when you have felt very motivated and fulfilled at work. What were you doing at those times? What about the work you were doing was fulfilling to you?

4. Think of times during your career when you have felt unmotivated and unfulfilled by your work. What were you doing at those times? What about the work you were doing was not a fit for you?

5. How do you feel about the work you are currently doing? How do you feel when Monday morning comes? What parts of your job bring you joy? Are there any aspects that are less satisfying for you?

6. Reflect back on the values you identified as being important to you in Chapter 3. How do these play out in your work?

7. What changes could you make right now to increase your level of fulfillment on the job? Are there stretch assignments or projects you could request? Could you craft your job to include more parts that are fulfilling to you? Could you make a mental shift in terms of how you perceive the work you are doing? Are there ways you can incorporate what you feel you were meant to do into your current role?

8. Is your current job or the culture of your organization too misaligned with your perceived purpose? For your own fulfillment, do you need to start looking into doing something else?

9. What one commitment can you make to yourself right now to make your work more meaningful to you?

These are some deep questions, and if you are unable to answer them on your first go-round, do not fret. As was the case with answering the self-awareness questions, developing a sense of purpose is a process. Tuck the questions away, reflect on them for a period, and write the answers in your journal. Over time, you will have new insights that will enable you to fine-tune your understanding of what is important to you, and how your work aligns with it. Armed with that knowledge, you will be able to move forward in ways that will allow you to create a more gratifying and engaging work life.

EBENEZER SCROOGE AND LEADERSHIP

We're on this planet for too short a time. And at the end of the day, what's more important? Knowing that a few meaningless figures balanced—or knowing that you were the person you wanted to be?

—Sophie Kinsella

Charles Dickens' novella, *A Christmas Carol*, is a classic text because of its deep and universal message. In the story, the miserly Ebenezer Scrooge is the recipient of some paranormal activity that forces him to look back on the choices he has made in his life and the associated legacy he will leave. As a result of his experiences, he transforms his life, moving from being "a squeezing, wrenching, grasping, scraping, clutching, covetous, old sinner" to a kind, benevolent, and compassionate man.

The impetus for Scrooge's metamorphosis came as a result of being faced with the prospect of his own death. Existential psychologists call this process *death awareness*. They argue that thinking about our eventual demise is not an exercise in morbidity; instead, it can be a source of great motivation. By reflecting on the fact that our time on earth is limited, it can create a sense of urgency in our lives to do the things we know, deep down, we should be doing to be fulfilled.

Most of us do not think much about our deaths as we go through our day-to-day existence. We focus on our schedules and the obligations that fill them; or perhaps we think about the positive aspects of our lives such as our kids, an exciting project, or a recent accomplishment. Most of the time, many of us have a "trees" view, as opposed to a "forest view" of life. As noted earlier, finding a sense of meaning and purpose in one's life requires taking a broader perspective, and any instance that can cause us to shift the lens through which we look at our lives can be beneficial.

As such, *boundary experiences* are occurrences that can frequently provoke us to think about our limited time on earth. By definition, a boundary experience is anything that causes us to consider our finiteness. For example, we have heard stories of the man who turns fifty and decides it is finally time to pursue his dream of getting a pilot's license. Or the woman who is diagnosed with diabetes and decides to make the changes to live a healthier lifestyle. Or the man who is unexpectedly served with divorce papers who changes his ways and puts more focus on his relationships. Milestone birthdays, major life transitions, illness diagnoses, and tragedies are classic examples of events that cause many of us to take a moment to reflect on our life circumstances.

Instead of waiting for a boundary experience to occur, a consummate leader can take a more active stance with respect to exploring death awareness. Take your time and work your way through the exercise below to reflect on this important concept.

Death Awareness Exercise

1. If you were to die tonight, what would your obituary say? Write it as honestly as you can, based on how you are currently living your life. (Assume it is not an obituary filled with euphemisms and niceties written by a grieving loved one. Instead, create a starkly candid version, written by an objective party).

2. How did it feel to write this? What feelings did it bring up for you?

3. Now assume you get a "do-over." In an ideal world, what would you like your obituary to say? What would you like your legacy to be? (As you write it, try to keep it realistic. So, for example, if you are 48, it is unlikely you will win an NBA Championship. It should feel like a stretch, but achievable).

4. How did it feel to write this version of your obituary?

5. Based on this exercise, what changes (if any) do you need to make in your life to live with a greater sense of purpose? What commitment can you make to yourself to start the process this week?

HELPING OTHERS TO FIND MEANING

Given that we know the importance of finding a sense of meaning and purpose at a personal level, it is probably not surprising to consider that a consummate leader is one who is skilled at helping her people perceive a sense of purpose in their roles. Cranston and Keller[9] call this being attentive to work's "meaning quotient" (MQ), as it can help people be more likely to achieve a state of being "in the zone" at work. They argue that when the MQ in an organization is low, it puts people more in the mentality of seeing their work as a *job* as opposed to a *calling*.

One strategy they espouse for creating more meaning at work is to inspire people by making sure you are conveying a variety of perspectives when trying to rally the troops – by "telling five stories at once." In their research they found that in their attempts to inspire others, organizational leaders tend to focus solely on the effect an initiative will have on the company. Thus, they provide motivational tales of how by working hard, they can all turn around a struggling organization, or else perhaps take an average company from good to great. The problem is, however, that this sort of approach is meaningful to only 20% of the population.

Thus, the additional "stories" they suggest leaders tell to inspire others to find a sense of meaning in work are discussing the effect an initiative will have on:

(1) society (such as by positively influencing the community)

(2) the customer (such as by bettering their quality of life or providing them with quality service)

(3) the work team (such as creating a cohesive environment)

(4) the individual (such as by providing opportunities for learning or for more compensation)

Since the researchers found about 20% of their sample was motivated by each of these areas, by covering all of these topics, a leader can ensure she is speaking in a language that will resonate with everyone.

I also recommend helping employees to find meaning in their work by enabling them to see how their role fits into the big picture. Just as the hospital cleaners who saw their jobs as contributing to patient care and the running of the hospital felt greater empowerment and engagement, others can also be encouraged to see their roles in a different light. When delegating tasks to those who work for you, make sure to highlight the importance of what they are doing so they can feel a greater sense of pride in their work.

Finally, make a habit of setting an inspiring vision of abundance for people that speaks both to their hearts and minds. Think of Martin Luther King's "I Have a Dream" speech. At the time, the future for which he was advocating was incredibly audacious, yet it spoke to people and created a compelling picture of what could be possible. It's also crucial that once you have painted the vision – as Dr. King did – you back it up with your actions. For example, if you say "we're going to innovate" and then proceed to shoot down every new idea someone brings to the table, you are likely to suck the energy and sense of meaning from people. Instead, internalize your sense of purpose and lead the way for your people.

A leader is one who knows the way, goes the way, and shows the way.

—John C. Maxwell

MY STORY

On a personal level, my career has provided me with lots of grist for the mill in terms of understanding the process of finding a sense of purpose in life and work. In graduate school, I earned a doctorate degree in clinical psychology, and as part of my training, I had the opportunity to work with individuals dealing with a variety of serious psychological issues, including depression, anxiety, schizophrenia, bipolar disorder, eating disorders, abuse, relationship strife, and the like. I taught undergraduate courses in psychology and conducted research on various issues related to African Americans. I enjoyed working with individuals of various levels of functioning, helping them to develop, alleviate symptoms, and live more fulfilling lives.

In the midst of my postdoctoral fellowship at the Emory School of Medicine, I was exposed to the world of corporate consulting. I had never heard of corporate psychology before, and I must admit that even though I was a little intimidated by the idea of transitioning from conducting therapy with predominantly low-income individuals with serious and persistent mental illness at a public hospital to providing advice to CEOs, there were also some intriguing aspects to this opportunity. The idea of travel, sitting in boardrooms, and making much more money than I had envisioned myself making as a therapist all seemed to tip the scales in favor of at least investigating this potential job opportunity. So, I threw caution to the wind, applied for the position, and much to my surprise, was selected by my firm to be a corporate psychologist.

As one may expect, I experienced a good deal of culture shock in my first few months in the role. While I had always been used to being in the minority in my surroundings (I grew up in a small town in Western Canada), in the corporate setting, I was in the minority in practically every imaginable way. In addition to being the only racial minority in the room 99 out of 100 times, I was also usually the only woman, as well as the youngest in the room, sometimes by twenty or more years. In addition, I had to adjust to a "corporate mindset."

While my graduate training as a therapist had taught me to look for the nugget of goodness in everyone, the corporate world required a much more tough-minded stance. For example, I was often being paid to recommend how well senior executives were suited to certain roles, and at times, I had to communicate the conclusion that they would likely not meet their employers' expectations. Initially, I felt that I was being "mean" making such recommendations, and I genuinely wondered what I had gotten myself into. The pace of the corporate world was much quicker than the pace in academia, and I found the ultimate goal of my job – "making businesses more money" – that was frequently communicated to me to be somewhat unsatisfying.

I toyed with the idea of going back into doing therapy – hanging out my own shingle, getting on an insurance panel, and attracting clients. Yet, I had become accustomed to the comforts of a generous salary with bonuses and had some fear about being able to earn enough money to maintain my lifestyle as a single woman (and the associated mortgage, car note, and student loan payments). In addition, I was aware that I might have been imagining the grass to be greener on the other side of the fence, romanticizing my previous work as a therapist and conveniently forgetting about issues like worrying about potentially suicidal clients, dealing with uncooperative insurance companies, and the fatigue associated with being compassionate and present all day long without any opportunity for taking breaks. Thus, despite fantasies of moving on to "bigger and better" things (and even actually writing a resignation letter at one point), I eschewed making a bold move and soldiered on, feeling a sense of dissatisfaction and ennui with my work.

As mentioned in the book's introduction, an unexpected breakup in my personal life spurred me on to do some spiritual exploration. In a sense, I started to try to answer the question of "Why am I here?" My answer changed the course of my life and work.

As noted, I had always felt some degree of discomfort with my work as a consultant. I felt I was good in the role, but I also knew that I lacked deep passion for the work I was doing. At times, I would compare myself to one of my colleagues who conducted employee engagement surveys and seemed truly energized by his work, or another colleague who led team-building sessions with enthusiasm and aplomb. In contrast, I felt like I was going through the motions, putting on a consultant "persona" but lacking a true sense of passion.

Then it finally hit me – I was not conducting my work in alignment with what I viewed as my purpose. I was being a consultant in the way others believed I should be, but as I was doing it, I wasn't tapping into anything that was particularly meaningful to me. Throughout my life, one of my goals has always been to help others to live happier, more productive, fulfilling lives. While I felt that financial prosperity was definitely a potential outcome for my clients, having that as the be-all-and-end-all goal simply wasn't satisfying enough to me. I reflected on my strengths and saw that I was only partially using them in some cases, and actually muting them in many instances.

I realized that I didn't have to approach my work as my colleagues were approaching it. Instead, I could use my interest in humanistic and positive psychology, along with my desire to explore deeper meaning with individuals, in the work force. I could fulfill my purpose of teaching people how to live fuller, self-actualized lives, and how to apply these lessons in the workplace. I knew this approach was somewhat different from a "typical" methodology, yet it felt right in the core of my being. What's more, I knew that I was the person who could do it. It would be different, yes, but I no longer had to constrain myself with the safety of being like everyone else.

I started off simply by creating a blog where I wrote posts about my ideas. I did it whenever I felt struck to do so, and it provided a small outlet for making me feel as though I was positively affecting the world with my ideas. (In reality, I was probably only influencing my family, as they were the only subscribers for the longest while!) Then, the idea came to me to develop a new endeavor in which I drew on the tenets of positive psychology to help businesses achieve greater performance outcomes. I knew that a lot of the companies with which I worked didn't view the work world in the ways that I was suggesting, yet I also knew there was a lot of compelling research that could potentially pique their interest.

The birth of my son (a boundary experience) provided the catalyst for me to make the leap. One day, as I looked into his eight-week-old face and told him he could be anything he wanted to be, it struck me that I wasn't living up to what I was telling him. I knew that to set the sort of example I wanted to, I needed to take more action to move toward my dream.

Scary as it was, I talked with my boss about a desire to approach my work differently. Surprisingly (as I thought that would be the end of the road for me), my boss asserted that he didn't want me to leave and encouraged me to devote three days a week to the activities of my firm, while also devoting two days a week to my new endeavors. This proved to be a wonderful arrangement for me and my family, and in my view was a form of divine intervention to reinforce my step of taking a risk.

With a deep sense of purpose, I listened to my intuition and took some risks so that I could learn and grow more quickly. For example, I signed myself up for an improv comedy class as a means of improving my presentation skills. As a card-carrying introvert, it was terrifying at times, but I pushed myself to do it, armed with the knowledge that it would put me in a better position to excel in work I found personally meaningful. I led workshops in the community to prepare me for presenting my work on a larger scale. I began writing this book as a means of sharing all the knowledge I had gained in my personal life and work, with people I hoped would benefit from it.

And what happened? Well, the results are obviously still being determined. On a personal level, finding a sense of purpose has given me a renewed energy and enthusiasm for my work. As Confucius said, "Choose a job you love, and you will never have to work a day in your life."

I can definitely say this was true for me. With a job I loved and believed in, I experienced new levels of inspiration. I woke up with creative ideas; I mentally developed presentations during my commute. I was even more driven to put my nose to the grindstone to gain a healthy and balanced lifestyle, because I wanted to embody what I was teaching. I was also more motivated to go out and land new clients, embracing the passion for the work I was doing. My enthusiasm and energy showed through, making developing business much more rewarding than it had previously been for me. I received referrals through word of mouth, and I achieved successes much more quickly than I had anticipated, all because I asked myself the questions, "Why am I here?" and "What is my purpose?"

While the dramatic stories of people leaving everything to pursue their dreams are the ones likely to become interest stories on television, I think my story is more typical. I didn't have to make a huge career change to enjoy a greater sense of purpose. I remained a corporate psychologist, but I made a slight shift in terms of my outlook and approach. As a consummate leader, you too will need to have a deep sense of purpose and meaning in your work. The associated self-exploration is well worth the effort.

> *Everyone has his own specific vocation or mission in life; everyone must carry out a concrete assignment that demands fulfillment. Therein he cannot be replaced, nor can his life be repeated, thus, everyone's task is unique as his specific opportunity to implement it.*
>
> —Viktor E. Frankl

CHAPTER FOUR

SELF-MANAGEMENT

The first and best victory is to conquer self.

—PLATO

As part of my graduate school training, I completed a predoctoral internship as an early-stage therapist at an Ivy League counseling center. This was a great opportunity for me to hone my skills, working with bright and talented students who needed some assistance dealing with challenges in their lives while in a high-pressure and competitive environment. During the fall semester, I had a client named Brandon who was one of my most trying cases that year.

Brandon came to me seeking help for social awkwardness and the feelings of anxiety he had about making friends, approaching women, and dating in general. He was a highly intelligent graduate student who was academically successful in his engineering program and reasonably well adjusted in most facets of his life. He was also incredibly self-aware. In fact, Brandon was so introspective that I'm sure he could not only provide a brief thesis in response to each question I outlined in the previous chapters, he could likely also suggest several more questions for further contemplation! Brandon was skilled at analyzing his every action, his motives behind each action, and everything in his childhood that led to his entire repertoire of behaviors.

To many, I'm sure Brandon sounds like a therapist's dream. After all, he was a psychologically minded therapy devotee who faithfully came week after week, after having spent a good deal of time reflecting on my insights between sessions. Unlike some other clients, I never had to worry about random suicide threats in the middle of the night, risky behaviors, or squabbles about scheduling.

So why did Brandon try my patience more than any of my other clients? Because he was all bark and no bite, meaning he understood every nook and cranny of his psyche but was unwilling to do anything to make the changes he purportedly wanted to make. Week after week, I would give him assignments, and week after week he would return with a thorough analysis of why he had been unable to carry them out. After several months of this, I came to feel that his desired role for me was to be a friend who listened to him talk and make the odd suggestion, as opposed to being a therapist who helped him develop into a better version of himself. This was unbelievably frustrating for a young idealistic clinician like me who had hoped to save the world one person at a time through my therapeutic gifts.

In a nutshell, Brandon had self-insight to spare but nonexistent willingness to act. Like many of us, he understood several of the issues at play in terms of his personal psychology, but he simply couldn't (or wouldn't) take the steps to manage himself to achieve his goals. Learning how to manage yourself to effect positive change in your life is one of the hallmarks of a consummate leader, and it is to that topic I now turn.

MIND CONTROL

As a leader, understanding yourself and having a sense of purpose are only part of the battle. An equally important part is using your understanding to take action to develop for the better. Personal growth can require a good deal of courage. It requires a willingness to push yourself outside your comfort zone, experiment with new behaviors, make mistakes, learn from them, and repeat. As Calvin Coolidge said, "All growth depends upon activity. There is no development physically or intellectually without effort, and effort means work." Thus, the first step in being able to grow is to ensure you have a mindset that is conducive to development.

Research has shown the role our minds play in influencing outcomes. For example, in medical and psychological research, the gold standard is to run "double-blind" studies. A study is double-blind when neither the researcher nor the study participants are informed as to which research condition they are in. So in drug trials, for example, research subjects receive either an active pill or a placebo (an inactive pill). In a double-blind study, neither the subject nor the experimenter knows whether the pill he or she is taking is the drug or the placebo. This standard is in place because it has been found that if a researcher knows someone is in the experimental condition,

CHAPTER FOUR ⋎ SELF-MANAGEMENT

their expectations can subtly influence the outcomes (even if they are not attempting to do so).

Similarly, the placebo effect is another indication of the power of our mindset to affect outcomes. Studies have consistently shown that a segment of the control group (who have been given the placebo) shows improved outcomes. In other words, the mere expectation of getting better causes some people's illness, depression, or other malady to abate. Researchers frequently view the placebo effect as somewhat of a nuisance that needs to be controlled when conducting statistical analyses or designing a study. However, in my view, the placebo effect is powerful evidence of the influence of our minds on co-creating our realities.

Stanford psychologist, Carol Dweck, has conducted extensive research about how one's mindset affects her view of the world and the results she is able to achieve in life.[11] She argues that in any given area, individuals can have one of two mindsets: a fixed mindset, or a growth mindset. Those with a fixed mindset believe that skills in any given area are innate and cannot be changed. They believe you are born intelligent, athletically gifted, or socially skilled. If you weren't fortunate enough to be born with those qualities, you're simply out of luck. In the work world, for example, they believe that strong salespeople bring in customers effortlessly, leadership skills are natural, and charisma is something a lucky few with the "it factor" exude instinctively.

Individuals who possess a growth mindset look at the world very differently. They believe that skills can be learned and that, through effort, one can become better in any chosen area. Therefore, with determination, you can become more intelligent, athletic, or socially skilled. You can get training to improve your sales skills, develop into a great leader, or inspire people through your charisma.

As you might expect, research has shown that people with these contrasting mindsets behave very differently. For example, Dweck conducted a study with elementary school students in which they were given relatively easy jigsaw puzzles to complete. After successfully completing the puzzle, those with the fixed mindset were more likely to choose to redo easy jigsaw puzzles, whereas those with a growth mindset chose to challenge themselves with more difficult ones.

Another study was done with college students who had done poorly on a test. After receiving the results, they were given the option to study tests of other students. Those with a growth mindset were more inclined to study exams of students who had done far better than they had so they could learn from them. Conversely, students with a fixed mindset chose to look at the tests of students who had done poorly so they could feel better about themselves.

Mindsets can also be induced in others by how they are instructed or reinforced. In another study with children, Dweck and her associates gave them some relatively difficult problems to solve. They praised some children by telling them they were smart (instilling a fixed mindset), while praising others for the amount of effort they had put in (growth mindset). Next, they were offered a challenging new task. As expected, the fixed-mindset children were much less likely to want to take it on as compared to the growth-mindset children. After their initial successes, both sets of children described the task as enjoyable; however, after being given challenging activities, the fixed-mindset group said it wasn't fun anymore. Interestingly, when they were given the opportunity to write out their thoughts on the exercise for other kids and report their scores, 40% of the fixed-mindset children lied about their scores.

Given the views of the two groups, these sorts of behaviors make perfect sense. If you have a fixed mindset and believe you either "have it or you don't," one of your primary goals will be to try to appear capable and competent. Thus, challenges are something you would be unlikely to seek out, since a failure would expose you as someone who is lacking in a given area. Witnessing others' success would be threatening, as it would remind you of your deficiencies. The safest option for someone with a fixed mindset is to stay in the box in which he has put himself, surrounding himself with mediocre people so that he can maintain his sense of confidence, no matter how fragile and tenuous it might be. Dweck argues that this sort of behavior will likely lead a person to underutilize his potential, since he's less likely to push himself. Ironically, this will further reinforce his perspective that he is inadequate.

In contrast, if you have a growth mindset and believe you can learn through effort, your goal is to improve as much as you can by putting in hard work. Instead of perceiving challenges as things to avoid, you willingly take them on, as you realize they are necessary to stretch yourself and grow. If you fail in a given area, you conclude that you need to work harder or figure out a strategy that is more conducive to success. You embrace being around others who are more skillful than you, because you can learn from them and be inspired by their successes. Through your hard work, you continue to grow and improve. This helps you maximize your potential and reinforces your perspective that through effort and a willingness to learn, you can develop your skills.

While much of the research related to fixed and growth mindsets has been done in educational settings, there have also been some studies done in the business world. For example, individuals with growth mindsets have been shown to be more effective at negotiating, probably because they are more likely to set high goals for themselves and to work hard when obstacles arise (as opposed to giving up when the going gets tough).[10] Thus, their level of motivation and the explanations they give themselves during a negotiation allow them to outperform their fixed-mindset peers.

Another study has shown that managers who have a growth mindset are more likely to invest time and effort into coaching their direct reports.[12] In addition, fixed-mindset managers who were taught about the importance of having a growth mindset when coaching employees exhibited a greater willingness to coach an underperforming employee, and gave better quality feedback compared to a control group of fixed-mindset managers.

Finally, in a study in which management groups were put together and given the task to run a simulated organization, the growth-mindset group outperformed the fixed-mindset group.[13] Because the members of the fixed-mindset group were more concerned about how they were coming across to their colleagues, they did not engage in the same open dialogue as the members of the growth-mindset group. In addition, the members of the growth-mindset group benefited more in response to mistakes by changing strategies and learning from errors.

It is important to point out that a fixed mindset isn't necessarily all pervasive; in other words, you can have a fixed mindset in one area and a growth mindset in another. For example, when I was growing up I believed that my intellect would enable me to learn anything if I put my mind to it (growth mindset), but I was convinced that I wasn't particularly athletic (fixed mindset). It wasn't until I reached adulthood and played tennis under an encouraging coach that I realized I actually was very athletic. Looking back, I recognize that given that I was one of the youngest kids in my class because I was born near the cutoff in August *and* skipped a grade, one would expect I would have been behind my peers in terms of my physical development. However, no one pointed this out to me! In the world of gym classes with track meets and grades, I was simply one of the slower, smaller ones, and I assumed this was simply because I wasn't good at sports. If I had been coached differently, I believe I would have understood that I could improve my own abilities, and that the standard I should have been aiming for was to outperform myself, instead of aiming for the Canada Fitness Guidelines set for an older child in my grade.

Take a moment to think about which mindset is more reflective of you by considering the following questions:

1. Are there certain areas in which you feel like you underperform?
2. Do you have a fixed or a growth mindset in those areas?
3. How could you behave differently to improve in those areas?
4. Are there certain challenges that deep down you know would be good for you, but you are afraid to put yourself out there and try them? Why?
5. How could you psych yourself up differently in those areas?
6. Has a past failure caused you to abandon a dream of yours? What can you learn from that failure?
7. Do you simply need to put in more effort or try a different strategy to address the failure?

Strive to be aware of your thinking and watch out for the traps of the fixed mindset. You will know you're in a fixed mindset when:

- you catch yourself being more concerned with looking good than taking on a challenge or developing in some way.
- you catch yourself becoming self-critical in response to a failure.
- you catch yourself being defensive or making excuses in response to your feedback.

Be kind to yourself, and reinforce the importance of learning in order to improve. Remind yourself of people like Winston Churchill who repeated a grade in school, or Thomas Edison's purported 10,000 attempts before successfully inventing the light bulb, to normalize the importance of persistence in accomplishing goals and achieving your full potential. Then, make a commitment to improve in an area in which you have a fixed mindset. You will be better for it.

As you are working on your own mindset, ensure that you are fostering a growth mindset in your teams. Try to avoid asking questions that will tend to shut down discussion and learning; strive also to avoid placing blame, being excessively critical, or putting people on the defensive. Instead, ask questions based on curiosity that promote learning and understanding. In addition, when highlighting results, make sure to reinforce progress and effort. And in those instances when people put in concerted effort but failed, emphasize their efforts while focusing on uncovering different strategies or approaches they could take in the future.

CHAPTER FOUR ⁜ SELF-MANAGEMENT

> *I always did something I was a little not ready to do. I think that's how you grow. When there's that moment of "Wow, I'm not really sure I can do this," and you push through those moments, that's when you have a breakthrough.*
>
> —Marissa Mayer

Recently, I saw an excellent contrast of growth versus fixed mindsets in the course of my work while conducting back-to-back feedback sessions with two individuals I had previously assessed. As you read their stories, see if you recognize yourself in either or both of the illustrations.

The first meeting was with Kerry, a woman in her mid-thirties who had just been hired for her first director position in a healthcare system. Only a few months into the position, Kerry had done an excellent job of acclimating herself to the organization and its mission-driven culture due to her outstanding interpersonal skills, strong insights into herself, and a knack for picking up on group dynamics. She was a hard worker who loved her job and was skilled at managing her own workload to get things done.

However, while she was an adept self-manager, she was less skilled at managing others due to her reluctance to address their lapses in performance. Her own self-doubt and desire to avoid potentially uncomfortable discussions caused her to give others more benefit of the doubt than was warranted, in the hopes that issues would resolve themselves.

A second developmental opportunity for Kerry was her tendency to dominate conversations because of her enthusiasm. Her husband joked that her energy sometimes wore him out, and she recognized that there was likely a segment of the work population who might have a similar reaction to her passion and effusiveness.

Once she had read through the report of my findings, Kerry asked questions to clarify and broaden her understanding of how her strengths and developmental opportunities played out. She acknowledged areas for growth and took pride in the assessment's validation of her strengths. She took copious notes throughout the session as we brainstormed about steps to include in her action plan, as well as ways she could utilize those around her to give her further feedback about her progress.

At one point, she caught herself speaking so much that she vowed to recruit others around her who could give her a discreet signal to alert her that it was time to "shut up!" She also requested a reading list so she could further her knowledge and skills. The session was interactive and positive, and Kerry left expressing gratitude for the opportunity to go through the process, feeling energized and optimistic about the future progress she would make through practice and hard work.

Feeling pumped and eager to continue the growth-fest, I invited in my next client, Linda, who had been brought into the organization to focus on patient safety. Linda brought a lot to her role: she was an exceptionally intelligent subject matter expert who possessed a great depth of knowledge in her field. She was even-tempered, helpful, and committed to accurate, high-quality work. She was able to articulately convey her thoughts and draw on her familiarity with the scientific literature to express to others the reasons for changing protocols.

One area of growth that came out of the assessment process was an opportunity for Linda to enhance her executive presence by moderating her tendency to be so private and reserved that it made it difficult for others to read her or to get close to her. Because her communication style was so logical and informational, she spoke to people's minds but not to their hearts. Thus, while her approach appealed to some, she had an opportunity to expand her impact by broadening her style. In addition, while her desire for accuracy was a strength, it could also work against her when it caused her to avoid speaking up or taking chances due to a desire to avoid making mistakes. Her reluctance to take risks limited her ability to market her ideas throughout the organization, and it frequently caused her to be overlooked in meetings.

Linda read through her report quickly, without taking notes, and said, "that was interesting." Recognizing she looked somewhat uncomfortable, I attempted to draw her out by encouraging her to talk about what felt good to read about herself. After a brief discussion about her intelligence and ability to get things done, and how she was performing well in her role, she said, "I think I've changed a lot since this was done."

I reinforced her for her developmental efforts and asked her about how she had grown since the assessment. She went on to catalogue how none of the developmental opportunities applied to her, as they hadn't been an obstacle to her getting things done in her role. Realizing she was caught up in thinking of developmental opportunities as weaknesses, I tried to reframe the concept by explaining that developmental opportunities are just as they are named, *opportunities* for growth. As an example, I talked about how Michael Jordan – arguably the greatest basketball player of all time – was clearly never hampered by his skills, but he still chose to work on the parts of his game that were relatively weaker so that he could continue to improve as a player and maintain his dominance throughout his career.

I also gently provided her with feedback, expressing that even as a psychologist, my own experience was that she was harder for me to read than most people, because she was a woman of few words and expressions. After acknowledging that she had heard that feedback before, she reiterated that it did not prevent her from getting her job done, and thus was not an issue. Finally, I diplomatically asked, "If none of these developmental opportunities apply to you, what *can* you focus on to enhance your growth?" At that point she got quiet, thought for a moment, and said, "I'm not sure."

I do not need to belabor the contrast, but I think it is clear that while Kerry approached the session seeking growth, Linda approached the session seeking to underscore her appearance as a competent professional. Providing Kerry with feedback was a rewarding experience; talking with Linda about her growth felt like an arduous chore. This suggests that Kerry will likely receive more coaching that will continue to help her grow, while Linda's resistance will likely impede others from providing her with potentially helpful feedback. And it doesn't take a rocket scientist (or even a psychologist) to predict that given their respective attitudes, Kerry will likely continue to blossom and grow as a leader, while Linda will, in all probability, stay about the same – despite her inherent advantages with respect to intellect.

I THINK I CAN, I THINK I CAN

Another concept that could be considered a close relative of Dweck's growth and fixed-mindset dichotomy is Albert Bandura's theory of self-efficacy.[14] Essentially, self-efficacy refers to your assessment of your ability to be successful in a certain area. If I have a high level of self-efficacy in a given area, I believe that I can achieve it. In contrast, if I have a low level of self-efficacy, I doubt my ability to succeed in that area. Self-efficacy beliefs have been shown to affect our behaviors and our thoughts, which in turn shape our effectiveness in our careers.

With respect to behaviors, if you have a high level of self-efficacy with regard to a certain task, you are likely to attempt it. Meanwhile, if your level of self-efficacy is low, you are more inclined to attempt to avoid it.

For example, if you believe in your ability to be successful taking on a project outside of your area, you are more likely to raise your hand and volunteer to take part in it. Conversely, if your level of self-efficacy with respect to that project is low, you are more likely to try to avoid being selected for the task. Research suggests that the optimum level of self-efficacy for any given task would be slightly above your level of ability, as it motivates you to take on tasks that will stretch you while still providing you with a high probability for success.

Self-efficacy also affects our thoughts. If your level of self-efficacy is low, you are likely to perceive tasks as being more difficult than they are. In contrast, if your level of self-efficacy is relatively high, you will perceive the task as achievable.

Self-Efficacy	Behaviors	Thoughts
High	Likely to attempt	Perceive tasks as achievable
Low	Likely to avoid	Perceive tasks as more difficult than they are

When obstacles arise, an individual with a high level of self-efficacy persists, believing that greater effort will lead to success. Their counterparts with low self-efficacy would be more prone to give up in these instances.

I have seen time and time again in my work how self-efficacy affects success. I have frequently come across individuals who have a great deal of innate talent, but simply don't believe in themselves. As a result, they don't take chances in their careers or put themselves out there, opting for security instead of taking smart, calculated risks that could bring greater success. By contrast, some of their less-skilled peers – but with a greater sense of self-confidence and self-efficacy – assertively introduce themselves to others in the organization and jump headlong into projects, resulting in greater opportunities to gain recognition and promotions. The key difference underlying these different career tracts is simply a belief in one's abilities.

Bandura argues there are a number of ways to increase your level of self-efficacy.[15] The first means of increasing it is to **gain experience** in a certain area, such as forcing yourself to move outside of your comfort zone to attempt a new activity. In taking on the new task, you may find that it was not as difficult as you had thought it might be, and as a result, you develop greater confidence in your ability to achieve it.

The key here is to ensure that the task you are taking on is one that is challenging, but still likely achievable for you. So, for example, if you wanted to improve your level of self-efficacy in tennis, you would not aim to take on Rafael Nadal in a match. Instead, you would sign up for your local rec league at a level that is commensurate to (or slightly above) your current level of ability.

Another means of improving self-efficacy is through **vicarious experience**. By observing someone similar to you succeeding in a given area, it can provide you with the motivation that "if he can do it, so can I." For example, I worked with a client who had wanted to lose weight to enhance her executive presence. However, no matter how hard she tried, she was unable to put in the sustained effort required to achieve her goal. As a result, she developed the belief that she was unable to lose weight. At one point, however, one of her colleagues (who was actually larger than she was) took up running and across time, that colleague lost 70 pounds. Inspired by the success of her coworker, she realized that if someone she knew (with whom she had previously eaten junk food) could succeed, so could she. Armed with greater determination and self-efficacy, she eventually achieved her weight-loss goals.

A third means of increasing self-efficacy is through *persuasion*. Talking yourself through a task can be an effective means of dealing with feelings of anxiety that may come up. As you talk to yourself, you can normalize the feelings and then persist on with the task. Having a trusted confidante or coach who can help you to troubleshoot, bolster your confidence, and encourage you as you stretch yourself can also be helpful in building self-efficacy. Again, the encouragement will enable you to have the experience, which in turn can further boost your level of self-efficacy.

Monitor yourself to determine those areas in which your self-efficacy is low. Then, follow the strategies for increasing it. This will allow you to broaden your horizons, learn new things, and become a more effective leader.

LESSONS FROM SPONGEBOB SQUAREPANTS

> *A pessimist sees the difficulty in every opportunity; an optimist sees the opportunity in every difficulty.*
> —WINSTON CHURCHILL

I have an eight-year-old nephew who, like a lot of kids his age, spends a good deal of time watching television. Thus, often against my will, I have found myself watching overly precocious kids on tween shows sassing adults and going on dates far before I think they are ready – and this is between commercials and music videos designed to sell said performers' albums. While those types of shows admittedly aren't my cup of tea, one of my nephew's shows that I actually find bearable is the cartoon *SpongeBob SquarePants*.

On the show, SpongeBob is a sea sponge who, with his various friends—Patrick, Squidward, and others—engages in various antics. While SpongeBob may not be the smartest of the creatures in Bikini Bottom, one quality he possesses is pure and utter optimism. Armed with his ability to see the silver lining in every situation, Bob's optimism can serve as a lesson for leaders.

Life as a business leader can be a challenging and stressful endeavor. There is a lot of pressure to remain profitable to keep shareholders, bosses, and boards happy and to ensure employees are able to be taken care of financially. The pace is quick and unexpected difficulties can frequently arise. Approaches that worked in the past don't always continue to produce the same results in the present. Just as Churchill's quote suggests, being able to remain resilient and to optimistically look for new opportunities when challenges arise is the hallmark of a consummate leader.

THE POWER OF OUR THOUGHTS

It is often said that what separates humans from other mammals is our ability to engage in higher cognitive processes. And while our ability to think things through can be an asset in terms of solving problems and considering abstract issues, our thoughts can also work against us. When was the last time you saw a cat who seemed to be thinking, "I'm not going to hunt any more birds. I tried the last time, and it didn't work out. Clearly I'm a failure"? Or, what about a dog thinking, "She may reject me. I'm not going to go over there and say hello"?

We humans, however, are notorious for such thoughts, and they act as the soundtrack that plays in our heads all day. While some of our thoughts work for us (e.g., "I'm killing this presentation!"), others can work against us (e.g., "I'll never be able to sell anything."). Unfortunately, for many of us, we experience these automatic thoughts and respond to them as if they are gospel truth. Instead of questioning their validity or examining the role they play in our lives, we simply act on them, allowing them to lift us up – or sabotage us.

In his classic book, *Learned Optimism*,[16] psychologist Martin Seligman notes that optimists and pessimists differ in three key areas in terms of how they explain events:

1. <u>PERMANENCE</u> – Pessimists tend to see negative events as permanent, whereas optimists are more likely to see them as temporary occurrences. Because optimists perceive negative events as simply part of the vicissitudes of life, they are more likely to bounce back quickly from disappointments. Conversely, when explaining positive events, optimists are more likely to see their causes as permanent, whereas pessimists see the causes of positive events as temporary. For example, in response to receiving a rejection of a sales proposal, an optimist may think, "This was not the right time for them to use our service." A pessimist may conclude, "I am never going to be able to sell this product to them."

2. <u>PERVASIVENESS</u> – A pessimist tends to generalize failures. Thus, a failure in one area of his life suggests that failures in other areas of his life are likely. An

optimist is more likely to compartmentalize failures; however, she is more prone to generalize positive events too. For example, in response to the sales failure, a pessimist may say, "I can't do anything right." An optimist may conclude, "I wasn't so good today. I need to practice this sales presentation again."

3. <u>PERSONALIZATION</u> – Optimists tend to see the causes of negative events as being outside of themselves, whereas pessimists blame themselves as the causes of disappointments. On the other hand, optimists tend to take credit for positive events, while pessimists see the causes as external. So, in our sales example, a pessimist may declare, "They just didn't like me," whereas an optimist would say, "They're just not in the mood to buy."

Seligman uses his A-B-C model to demonstrate how the explanatory style of optimists and pessimists has an impact on their behavior, and in turn, the results they achieve:

- **A** stands for antecedent event (or adversity).

  In essence, it is the event that causes us to make some sort of attribution.

- **B** stands for belief.

  The belief in any given situation is based on how we explain the event to ourselves (i.e., the associated thoughts).

- **C** stands for consequence.

  As a result of our belief, we have certain emotions and behaviors.

In a nutshell, our thoughts influence our behaviors, which affect the outcomes we experience. For example, if, based on a rejection in a sales situation, I conclude that "They didn't like me and I'm a failure," I'm probably not going to be running headlong into the next sales opportunity. Instead, I'll want to protect my dignity and focus on doing the things at which I feel competent. Taking this approach will prevent me from improving my sales abilities, and it will also reduce the likelihood of making more sales. By contrast, if I attribute a sales rejection to the fact that a customer simply wasn't interested in buying, I can feel confident as I approach my next prospect, knowing that the experiences are two independent events.

Consummate leaders' optimistic explanation styles enable them to maintain hope in the face of challenges, and to inspire those who work with and for them to perceive trials in a similar light. Their sense of optimism enables them to take some risks (it should be noted that blind optimism isn't the goal, but rather an upbeat and positive perspective), after having anticipated possible drawbacks. When failures occur (and they inevitably will for anyone who is pushing the envelope in terms of innovation), they are able to dust themselves off and "get back on the horse," having learned from their mistakes.

Becoming More Optimistic

If, upon self-reflection, you determine that you are someone who could benefit from developing a more optimistic approach, you are in luck. As Seligman's book title suggests, optimism can be learned. Consummate leaders in the making who do not presently have a sunny disposition can learn to keep tabs on their thoughts and beliefs to make sure their cognitions work *for* them, as opposed to *against* them. Read on for a method to help you think more optimistically.

Become Aware of Your Thoughts

Instead of allowing your thoughts to arise unchallenged and letting them control you, start to notice your negative thoughts. Thus, over the next few weeks, be on the lookout for when you are engaging in pessimistic thinking. If you are used to looking at the world through negative eyes, it can be so automatic that you may not even realize you are doing it. Signs that may indicate you are doing so include feeling disappointed, depressed, discouraged, or stuck. When you notice yourself feeling this way, see if you can backtrack to the event and the thought that contributed to that feeling.

Once you have learned to identify your thoughts, you can start to work with them. For some people, it can be helpful to self-reflect on their thoughts to determine where they came from and how they affect them. For example, if you think to yourself, "If I'm not perfect, I'm a failure," it may help to gain insight as to where that thought originated.

- Did it come from a parent or a childhood coach?
- How does that thought affect your behavior in this particular instance?
- Do you have similar thoughts in your daily life?
- How do they affect how you behave?

While understanding the origins of your thoughts can be helpful in terms of gaining self-awareness and insight, an additional step is usually necessary to develop a more optimistic explanation style. To learn to think more optimistically, Seligman recommends keeping an ABCD journal. We discussed the A, B, C previously; however, the D refers to disputation, or the practice of challenging one's pessimistic beliefs to develop a more optimistic perspective. This is not a matter of becoming a Pollyanna who views the world through rose-colored glasses. Instead, Seligman describes it as "non-negative thinking," or essentially, developing a perspective that is more constructive for success and growth. So, you are not responding with an affirmation (e.g., "Everybody loves me"); you are responding with a statement that is non-negative, but plausible.

For example, in the following scenario you reach out to a client who has not responded to your call in a week. Working through the A-B-C-D process, the outcome could be as follows:

> **Adversity** = Client does not respond to call
>
> **Belief** = "I'm no good at sales. I can never bring in new clients."
>
> **Consequence** = Feel discouraged and avoid trying to reach out to client
>
> **Disputation** = "One person not calling me back doesn't mean I'm not a good salesperson. There are any number of reasons that could explain why she hasn't returned my call. Let me try again."

In this next scenario, you make a presentation at work and receive a less-than-desirable response:

> **Adversity** = Lukewarm reception to your presentation
>
> **Belief** = "I can't do anything right. Now I'll never be considered for vice-president."
>
> **Consequence** = Feel dejected and reluctant to volunteer for another presentation
>
> **Disputation** = "One lukewarm presentation doesn't mean I'll never advance. In fact, I saw a vice-president make a mediocre presentation last month. I'm going to ask my boss for feedback so I can be better next time."

If you work your way through the disputation process consistently, you will find that over time it becomes more automatic. Eventually you may get to the point at which your belief is replaced by an optimistic one, negating the need for any disputation. Getting a handle on your thoughts is critical for becoming a consummate leader and developing the resilience you will need to perform at your peak.

As the explanations you give yourself become more optimistic, you will likely find that the explanations you provide those around you will similarly become more positive. Instilling others with a sense of hope and optimism as a leader is an important part of motivating people, and encouraging them to move on from disappointments to challenge themselves. Therefore, be intentional about using an optimistic explanatory style with your people.

CALGON, TAKE ME AWAY!

The consummate leader takes a holistic approach to leadership, understanding that attention to one's body, mind, and spirit results in the best outcomes. Up to this point, we have focused on mind and spirit. Now, we will explore how a focus on the body is critical for peak performance.

While consummate leaders recognize the importance of managing their time, they know that this is only the first step. They understand that equally important is the concept of managing their energy. After all, if you carve time out of your schedule to complete a task but don't have the energy to actually commit to doing it well, you are not managing yourself effectively.

Consummate leaders are cognizant that learning, growing, and positively affecting the world all require energy and activity. Without an appropriate self-care regimen, most individuals simply don't have the stamina to fully actualize their potentials, even if they set aside the time to do so. Instead of viewing self-care as a luxury they cram into their schedules when they can find the time, consummate leaders understand the importance of taking care of themselves, and as such, make it a priority in their schedules. While I encourage you to explore some of the excellent resources devoted to self-care listed in the recommended reading and viewing list in the back of the book, I will highlight three key activities I suggest all leaders incorporate into their schedules to perform at their peaks.

Exercise

You would have to be living under a rock not to know the benefits of regular exercise in contributing to a healthy lifestyle and overall wellness. In addition to the physical benefits it provides, it is an excellent mood regulator and stress reliever.

Exercise has also been shown to possibly contribute to neurogenesis, the creation of new nerve cells in the brain. In one study, after engaging in a three-month exercise regimen, participants showed a 30% increase in blood flow to the hippocampus (the part of the brain associated with memory and learning).[17] Other studies have shown that after exercise, subjects learned vocabulary words 20% faster than they did before exercise, and creativity improved after a mere 30 minutes on the treadmill.[18] In addition, office workers who exercised at lunchtime were found to be more productive, more in control of their workloads, and less stressed than those who didn't.[19] The bottom line is, not only is exercise good for your body, it also benefits your brain and your ability to do your job.

In terms of managing energy, I'm sure all of us have had the experience of a trip to the gym providing a bit more spring in the step. Personally, I have forced myself to go to the gym many times after a long day of work simply because I knew it was good for me. And every time (okay, almost every time), my efforts on the elliptical trainer or smith machine have been rewarded with increased energy and a feeling of self-satisfaction.

The consummate leaders I have worked with make exercise a regular part of their schedules, particularly when the demands of their jobs increase. They don't use their busy schedules as an excuse for skipping a trip to the gym; instead, they know it will provide them with a much-needed break from the stress of their jobs. Ideally, you should commit to exercising six days a week for at least 45 minutes at a time. However, if that is too much for you, then do whatever you are able, as even a little will provide you with some benefit.

Healthy Diet

What would a well-rounded lifestyle be without a healthy diet? Eating a variety of colorful, natural foods (skittles don't count) provides leaders with the energy they need to perform. Thus, working through lunch and grabbing something from the vending machine at 3:00 is out of the question. Instead, eating several small meals throughout the day creates the best outcomes.

In fact, there is fascinating research demonstrating that eating throughout the day helps contribute to self-control.[20] Studies show that when we are drawing on our willpower by making decisions or engaging in complex mental tasks, the body uses glucose for fuel. And, when glucose is depleted, we become less effective.

For example, without adequate glucose in our systems, we tend to become more complacent when making decisions, opting for the status quo instead of engaging in the problem solving needed to make the best choice. We are also less able to control our emotions, making us more prone to uncharacteristic outbursts. When glucose is depleted, we can become more impulsive as well, such as spending money unwisely or bingeing on unhealthy foods.

Consider the demands of a typical leader's day, which is chock-full of times that require self-control. Important decisions about organizational strategy need to be made. Mundane administrative tasks like expense reports have to be completed. Mouths need to be kept shut at opportune times to avoid getting fired. All of these are classic drains on glucose, leaving one at risk for a whole host of dysfunctional behaviors.

To guard against this, your goal should be to eat a balanced diet, including a healthy breakfast, low-glycemic index foods (basically, non-processed foods), and adequate calories. Eat every few hours to maintain your glucose and energy levels, and you will set yourself up to have your best performance.

MEDITATION

What exercise does for the body in terms of strengthening it and putting it in a better position to perform in demanding circumstances, meditation does for the mind. Want an increased ability to concentrate?[21] Meditation has that covered. Want to be in a better mood more often?[22] Meditation does that too. Want to be less susceptible to stress?[23] Meditation can help you out. Want to deepen your spirituality? Meditation often plays a role in that as well. Want to decrease the chances of getting sick?[24] You got it, meditation has your back.

Meditation is a virtual panacea for all that ails you. It has been shown to increase activity in your left prefrontal cortex, the portion of the brain associated with positive emotion. It has also been linked to reduced grey matter in the amygdala, the part of the brain associated with stress and fear.[25] Meditators are better able to regulate their emotions, concentrate, bounce back from setbacks, and listen to others.[26] Those sound like some attractive qualities in a skillful leader, don't they?

When I mention meditation to clients, some look at me incredulously and state flatly, "I could never do that. I'm far too Type A. I don't see myself sitting still for more than five minutes." Others admit, "I tried that. I'm no good at it. I couldn't make my mind go blank." What they fail to realize is that meditation does not require clearing one's mind and stopping all thoughts; it simply means gently observing one's thoughts nonjudgmentally when they come up and allowing them to drift away, instead of becoming obsessed with or attached to them.

It is beyond the scope of this book to delve too deeply into a meditation practice (there are a lot of valuable tomes dedicated to it),[27] but I do want to stress that anybody can learn to meditate. Meditation is referred to as a practice because it requires just that – consistent effort to enhance one's skill. The purpose of it is learning to be still so you can better notice what is going on within yourself. That is it. You are not expected to achieve enlightenment through the practice. If you do, more power to you, but that is not the goal. In fact, I have heard some meditation instructors say (somewhat cheekily, but accurately) that the goal of meditation is to just sit there.

If you think of it as exercise for the mind, and resist the pressure of thinking you have to achieve nirvana, you should have better results. And don't intimidate yourself by thinking that you have to sit for an hour. Whatever you can do to slow down, be still, and focus within will benefit you. Explore the different types of meditation through reading and finding local facilities in which to practice with others in person. Then, determine the style(s) that feels most comfortable for you. Your leadership skills, concentration, and focus will likely benefit as a result.

Developing a Meditation Practice

Here are some brief and simple steps to develop a meditation practice.

1. To start, set aside 5–10 minutes a day for practice. You might consider investing in a meditation timer. There are plenty of free or inexpensive apps you can download for this purpose, such as The Mindfulness App, Meditate, Mindfulness Meditation, and Buddhist Meditation Trainer. (I have found that using a timer prevents me from meditating with one eye open to track how much time has passed).

2. Find a pleasant, quiet place away from distractions. Put yourself in a comfortable position. For some, sitting cross-legged on the floor on a meditation pillow is most relaxing. For others, sitting in a chair is best. You may also choose to lie down, though that may make you more prone to fall asleep. Strive to have an erect posture. You may put your hands gently in your lap, or perhaps with your palms facing upward. There are a variety of possible hand positions in meditation, and I encourage you to explore this through your reading. Ultimately, your goal should be to select a position in which you feel relaxed, yet alert.

3. Close your eyes or focus softly on something in front of you. While closing your eyes may make you sleepy, meditating with your eyes open may make you more prone to being distracted. For most people with whom I have worked, closed eyes feel the most comfortable. You may choose to experiment with both approaches.

4. Breathe slowly and naturally. Focus on the sensation of your breath moving in and out of your body. Some people choose to count their breaths, perhaps up to ten, then start over from one again. Others may use a mantra (Hindu for "word"), such as "Om." You may say your mantra out loud or silently to yourself, or, you may choose to do none of the above and simply be silent. Mantras and counting can be helpful for providing you with something upon which to focus your thoughts.

5. When your mind wanders (and it invariably will), gently focus your attention back to your breath. You might choose to use imagery to deal with distracting thoughts. For example, you can imagine the particular thought being put on the wings of a butterfly and quietly being taken away. Or perhaps you can imagine the thought drifting away on a leaf in a gentle stream. However, if this sort of imagery creates further distraction for you, then simply let the thought go and return to your breathing.

6. One of the underlying principles of meditation is that no judgment is involved. Therefore, be very gentle on yourself in the process. Negative thoughts such as, "I can't believe I'm getting distracted again," or "I knew I wasn't good at this," will not serve any purpose while

meditating (except for, perhaps, giving you a greater sense of self-awareness regarding the sorts of things you say to yourself). Conversely, even positive thoughts like, "Wow, I'm totally getting this meditation thing!" are not aligned with a classic meditation practice. Your goal should be to become a neutral observer of your thoughts. Gently notice them, then let them go.

Once you have finished your practice, take a moment and notice how you feel. If, initially, five minutes seems too long, then start with two. Your goal should be to sit for whatever length of time to which you can commit. Given all the benefits associated with meditation, it is worth it to persist. Over time, you can gradually lengthen your practice.

READY, SET, GO!

The final aspect of self-management is taking action. As was the case with Brandon, all the knowledge in the world will do nothing for you if you don't apply it. To develop, you need to have a growth mindset, increase your level of self-efficacy, and be willing to take some risks. Understand that new behaviors will frequently feel uncomfortable. Getting comfortable with being uncomfortable should be your goal – it is the only way in which you can grow.

Just as a muscle increases in strength by being challenged, so too do you need to be challenged to develop personally and professionally. And just as it can be helpful to work with a trainer who can push you more than you may be inclined to push yourself, it can be helpful to work with a coach to ensure you are taking action. If a coach is not in your budget, you can share your goals with a friend or colleague to provide you with some external accountability. Ensure your friend is supportive, but willing to challenge you.

While it can feel good to have someone who is an enthusiastic and understanding cheerleader for everything you do, that sort of person may not be the best for encouraging your growth or confronting you when you do not follow through on a commitment. Instead, choose someone who is willing to push you and give you candid feedback, as well as enthusiastic support for your successes. Having a team of individuals focused on helping you will hasten your development.

Lastly, be patient with yourself as you develop new skills. Using my four-month-old son, Blake, as an illustration, there are not a whole lot of things he can do on his own, yet he is learning. For example, every day we have him doing "tummy time." For those of you who are not parents, tummy time is just as it sounds, time during which he is put on his belly. Given that infants are now supposed to be placed on their backs when sleeping to avoid Sudden Infant Death Syndrome (SIDS), tummy time allows them to build strength in their shoulders and core, and it prepares them for crawling.

When we first exposed Blake to tummy time, he could not even lift his head by himself. He would squirm and make slight whining and complaining noises until we flipped him over to his preferred station on his back. With persistence, however, his strength increased. Now, he proudly holds up his entire upper body with his arms with a look of delight and pride on his face for what he has accomplished. He has the same attitude moving through the stages toward being able to sit up on his own. Though he can only sit erect while propped up, he – even as a baby – can see that he is in the midst of picking up a new skill. When he topples over to the side, he does not beat himself up, as it is simply a part of learning; instead, he clamors to be propped up again. We, as adults, would be wise to borrow from the instinctual mindset of babies in this regard.

As you take your own baby steps in your developmental journey, make sure to celebrate your successes. When mistakes occur, recognize them as part of the growth process. Use them as opportunities to learn or to develop new strategies. Nurture your growth mindset and value the learning process. Most of all, don't give up! With time and persistence, you can pick up new proficiencies and become a consummate leader.

Action is the foundational key to all success.

—PABLO PICASSO

CHAPTER FIVE

Positivity

*He who is not contented with what he has,
would not be contented with what he would like to have.*

—Socrates

I have a friend named Allison who is the executive director of a community-oriented non-profit organization. She possesses a lot of skills that serve her well in her job: she has a solid education that provides her with all of the technical knowledge she needs to guide her organization in the best strategic direction; she is a compassionate person who sincerely cares about the well-being of the clients she serves; and she is hardworking and loyal, putting in long hours to forward the agenda of the business. Her staff reveres her for her devotion and commitment.

However, despite her gifts and the important work she does, Allison has many complaints about her work environment. For example, fundraising is always a problem. The people in her organization are uncommitted and unprofessional. The broader societal context makes it harder for her to truly influence her clients. Younger people in the non-profit consistently bother her by suggesting that the organization do things like blogging and tweeting, which are activities that take time away from serving clients. To the average person, it would sound like Allison's work environment is pretty awful, yet even though I am her friend, I am somewhat skeptical.

In her previous job, Allison complained that her people simply didn't understand her. Her boss was disrespectful and the working conditions were unacceptable. In the job before that, she was underpaid and unappreciated. When she was in university, some of her classmates were hostile and her advisor was unfair. One could conclude that given the "bad luck" she had experienced, Allison needed to do a better job of selecting organizations and positions that were a good match for her. However, since she was the common denominator in each of these circumstances, my conclusion was that the odds were greater that she and her attitude were, in fact, the problem.

In listening to her leadership experiences, it was not surprising to me that one area Allison grumbled about consistently was that the people who worked for her were unmotivated and underachieving. After all, how inspirational could it possibly be to work for a pessimistic boss who shoots down new ideas faster than a gunslinger and is quick to point out what is wrong in a situation, often overlooking what is right? I knew that even if her staff was not composed of the best and brightest talent, her style was likely making the situation worse. Her negativity was the exact opposite of what was needed to be an outstanding leader.

POSITIVE LEADERSHIP

Throughout the research literature, the conclusion is clear: positive leaders create better results for their businesses. Studies show that people who are high in subjective well-being (i.e., are happy and positive) are more likely to head companies that have greater returns on investment, receive higher performance ratings from chairpersons of their boards, be evaluated positively by superiors, and have autonomous, meaningful, and varied jobs.[28] They are also more likely to be productive, close sales, and lead teams who find that their work climate fosters high performance.[29]

These findings make intuitive sense. I'm sure all of us have worked with or for an Allison at some point in our careers. Individuals like this can suck the life out of a discussion with one negative comment. They can likewise cause their employees to become overly cautious instead of engaging in innovation, for fear they will be punished, as opposed to supported, for taking risks. Because they tend to be stingy with positive reinforcement, their employees often feel unappreciated.

Consummate leaders, on the other hand, are upbeat and positive. Instead of focusing on the constraints in a situation, they focus on coming up with new solutions. Their sunny dispositions create a sense of safety for their teams, thereby fostering the sort of environment that allows people to be more creative. Rather than being pushovers, they address performance issues, but do so in a respectful way that allows individuals to feel that they have been fairly treated. Their can-do spirit and positive moods are infectious, spurring their teams on to do great things.

Thus, to be a consummate leader, you must work toward having a positive approach to leadership. And in order to achieve that, you must be a more positive person. As such, the foundation for more positive leadership is to first work on yourself so you can have a greater sense of subjective well-being.

COME ON, GET HAPPY!

> *A man without mirth is like a wagon without springs, in which one is caused disagreeably to jolt by every pebble over which it turns.*
>
> —HENRY WARD BEECHER

In working with clients over the years, I have found it fascinating that many executives approach the concept of leading with positivity with a sense of skepticism. While on the one hand they have seen people respond well to positive leaders, they worry that too much positivity will cause their employees to rest on their laurels and become complacent. As a result, I have sometimes heard positive leaders referred to as "Pollyannas" or "lacking in toughness." Individuals who are distrustful of taking a positive approach tend to see work as "serious business" and have difficulty accepting that a focus on fostering positive emotions can coexist with driving results.

To be clear, I want to reiterate that I am not suggesting leaders ignore underperformance or become positive to the point of delusion. What I am pointing out, however, is that empirical research tells us that positive emotion is a powerful factor involved in creating an environment that increases the odds people will flourish. Individuals can have their opinions, but research is research.

Thus, to work toward being a consummate leader, it is critical to engage in the sorts of behaviors that will make one more inclined to experience positive emotions. As human beings, we tend to process and react more strongly to negative emotions and events than to positive ones.[30] While this helps to keep us out of harm's way, it can skew our assessments of how negative a situation really is. For example, in one study, researcher Teresa Amabile found that negative setbacks exerted twice the level of influence over an individual's level of happiness at work in a day, when compared to positive steps forward.[31]

Because people tend to experience negative events so strongly, recent research has shown that we need to have more positive than negative emotions or experiences to truly flourish in life. While there has been some question about what exactly the ideal ratio should be,[32] the generally accepted rule of thumb from a variety of studies indicates that a 3:1 ratio of positive to negative emotions is the benchmark for truly flourishing in work and in life.[33] While that might not sound like a particularly tall order, in reality only about 17% of us make the cut in that category.[34]

Although it may seem that achieving and maintaining happiness is something that occurs fairly naturally, in actuality, some degree of effort and discipline is generally required to maximize our level of subjective well-being. Therefore, before I provide you with some tools to work to increase the frequency with which you experience positive emotions, let me provide you with a bit more information you can draw on so you will know why working toward happiness is a necessity for anyone who aspires to be a consummate leader.

JOY TO THE WORLD

In her "Broaden-and-Build" theory,[35] Barbara Fredrickson argues that from an evolutionary perspective, negative and positive emotions serve different functions. While both serve a purpose in the right doses at the right time, experiencing too much negative emotion can interfere with optimal functioning.

According to her theory, negative emotions typically arise in response to some sort of threat, and they have the purpose of narrowing one's attention. For example, imagine that during your daily walk from your car to the office, a ferocious lion jumps into your path. Immediately you are overtaken by fear, and your fight-or-flight response is activated. Your awareness becomes narrowed – you are in survival mode, entirely focused on the menacing animal in front of you. The blood rushes from your brain to your extremities, preparing you to run, hide, fight, or play dead.

While the narrowed attention associated with negative emotions is adaptive when being attacked by wild animals, in day-to-day life, it can work against you. For example, have you ever regretted anything you have done when you were angry? (Is there truly anyone who hasn't?) While it might have seemed like a great idea at the time to fire off that vicious email to your coworker who offended you, thirty minutes later, once you had calmed down, it didn't seem quite so prudent. That's because when your blood was boiling, your attention was narrowed, and in this case, you were focused more on fighting than on solving the problem in a constructive manner. Later on, after calming down, your attention broadened and all of a sudden you thought about the consequences of your actions on your relationship with her, and how your newly minted reputation as the resident hothead may negatively affect others' willingness to work with you in the future.

On the other hand, positive emotions like joy, curiosity, and interest broaden your perspective by encouraging exploration, learning, play, and open-mindedness, to name a few possible reactions. While this broadened perspective may not seem to have much of an effect in the short term, across time, the benefits of experiencing positive emotions accrue, or build upon themselves. So, for example, people who experience curiosity tend to explore, which gives them more things about which to be curious. Over time, this allows them to become better problem solvers because they have been exposed to a wider variety of situations or ideas, and as a result, they have learned more and gained enhanced knowledge and skills.

Psychologist Lynn Johnson explains that the process by which positive emotions affect our higher-level thinking is related to our "three brains": our reptile brain (thalamus and brain stem), mammal brain (the limbic system), and angel brain (neocortex).[36]

The **angel brain** is the portion associated with problem solving, making decisions, planning, and engaging in complex tasks. This part of the brain allows us to make decisions, think about consequences, and have perspective.

The **mammal brain** is our emotional brain. This portion is associated with negative instinctive emotions such as anger, fear, and anxiety, as well as more positive emotions such as love and curiosity.

Finally, the **reptile brain** becomes dominant when we feel we are under attack (e.g., our fight-or-flight part of the brain). This portion is guided by base instincts and becomes the driver when we feel we are under threat.

When we are stressed, our reptile brain takes control. It is focused on taking action, as opposed to thinking. This explains why when we feel threatened we often engage in behaviors that we otherwise wouldn't – our neocortex is acting as a quiet bystander while our more primitive instincts to fight or flee are running the show. Again, this provides support for the idea that we should aim to regulate our moods and strive to have more positive emotions; doing so allows us to be better problem solvers and make better decisions, which in turn help us to live more adaptive lives.

Beyond the implications for better work performance, there is also a great deal of research that provides additional reasons for pursuing positive emotions.[37] For example, happy people experience more satisfying and long-lasting marriages. Individuals who are higher in subjective well-being tend to be more successful and make more money; they are also healthier, with stronger immune systems and lower stress levels than their more dissatisfied peers. Happy people live longer, have more friends, and enjoy deeper relationships. What's more, those who experience more positive emotion also tend to be more creative and exhibit better self-control.

Research tells us that the majority of reasons that account for why employees quit are factors that can be influenced by their managers.[38] In addition to the 32% who leave for career advancement and different job opportunities, and the 20% who leave for lack of fit with the position, almost one-fifth leave due to management and the general work environment. Therefore, a leader who attends to the culture, environment, and learning opportunities is one who is less likely to experience unintended turnover.

Another reason that it is important for leaders to manage their moods is due to a concept called **emotional contagion**. In essence, this means that people's moods tend to synchronize with those around them. Have you ever had the experience of being in a neutral mood, and then after dealing with someone who was negative, your mood was brought down along with him? That is a result of emotional contagion. Leaders have to be especially careful about regulating their moods, as they have been found to have a disproportionate amount of influence on the mood of their work force.[39] That same study found that when leaders were in a positive mood, the people in their groups were in more favorable moods and worked more efficiently together.

In another interesting Yale management study,[40] students in a business simulation were given instruction by an actor playing the manager role in one of four ways: "cheerful enthusiasm," "serene warmth," "depressed sluggishness," or "hostile irritability." The groups that received their instructions in the first two positive ways were most effective, winning their teams more profit in the exercise.

Encouraging your people to develop strategies to generate more positive emotions can also create better outcomes. For example, one study found that call center employees who had started off the day in a negative mood rated their customers more negatively than those who had woken up in a positive mood.[41] Further, after speaking to a negative customer, they were less productive and more likely to take a break after the call compared to their more positive peers.

Research has also shown that customers are susceptible to emotional contagion in that their moods are influenced by the mood of the employee with whom they were interacting.[42] Interestingly, if the employee is only pretending to be in a good mood, the contagion does not tend to occur. Attending to issues such as these is important, because the interaction between customer and employee affects such things as the customers' perception of the quality of the service and their likelihood to recommend the business to a friend.[43]

Because we know emotions are contagious and that managers' emotions have an inordinate amount of influence on the emotions of their work force, it is critical that leaders try to stay upbeat and uplifting. All of this, of course, may seem like common sense to you; however, despite the research, I have found it difficult to convince some people about the benefits of focusing on helping others to experience more positive emotions.

For example, my friend, Bill, is less positive and upbeat than I am, and he has always maintained to me that he would have my level of my optimism and happiness if he had my life. I think many people share this view. They see someone who is happy and think, "Well, of course she's happy – look at her job" or "I would be walking around smiling too if I had her relationship."

Interestingly, however, research has also shown that happy people experience just as many painful events as their less happy peers. They deal with the same life challenges, but their positive attitude allows them to bounce back more quickly from obstacles and keep setbacks in perspective.[44] The key difference between those who flourish and those who do not is that the former experience more positivity in response to routine daily events. So, for example, they are more grateful after having received a kindness from someone, or more excited about having learned something new.[45] And, as we know, these benefits accrue over time. In other words, it is not the events that happen in their lives that make them happy; au contraire, their attitude and the happiness they experience contribute to the positive events that occur in their lives.

A FORMULA FOR HAPPINESS

While Bill would also argue that he is just naturally more pessimistic and there's nothing he can do about it, Sonja Lyubomirsky, a prolific researcher in the field of happiness, would argue otherwise. Lyubomirsky has developed a formula for happiness that provides us with a good framework for understanding it:[46]

$$\text{Happiness} = \text{Set Point} + \text{Life Circumstances} + \text{Volitional Activity}$$

She asserts that we all are born with a happiness set point, which is analogous to the concept of a weight set point. Just as some of us are genetically predisposed to having an easier time maintaining a lean weight than others, some of us are born happier than others. So, while Bill is partially right, Lyubomirsky theorizes that only about half of our happiness level is based on this set point.

She also argues that 10% of our happiness is based on life circumstances. I think we could safely say that it's easier to be happy if you have a roof over your head, a steady income, and your basic needs covered. While money doesn't necessarily buy happiness, there is a slight positive correlation between income and happiness (perhaps because one has more control, access, and options in one's life). However, the relationship is not linear, meaning that as an individual becomes richer and richer, income matters less and less in terms of improving his well-being.[47] Still, note again that only 10% of one's happiness level is related to these external factors.

The great news is that about 40% of happiness is based on volitional (i.e., voluntary) activities. This means that we have control over almost half of our happiness! Just as someone with a higher weight set point could choose to eat healthy foods and exercise consistently to manage her weight, so too could someone with a lower happiness set point consciously engage in various strategies to increase her level of happiness.

FORMULA FOR HAPPINESS

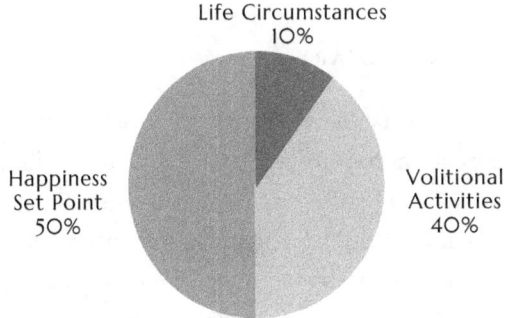

While Lyubomirsky suggests that these percentages may not be exact, the point is that we have control over a significant amount of our happiness. And if you aspire to be a consummate leader, you will take personal responsibility for flourishing as a means of being more effective as an individual performer and in leading others. Thus, it is essential to exercise the discipline necessary to do the sorts of things that will maximize your experience of positive emotions.

HAPPINESS TOOLBOX

He is a wise man who does not grieve for the things which he has not, but rejoices for those which he has.

—EPICTETUS

People experience the most enduring happiness when they serve others, are thankful and appreciative for what they have in their lives, and draw on their unique strengths and talents as they go about their lives. With that in mind, here are some tools you can use to increase the frequency of positive emotion in your own life.

The Gratitude Diary

The gratitude diary is a means of cultivating a greater awareness of all there is to be grateful for in your life. Instead of doing what people often do, which is to think about what they need to have or do to be happy in the future, the gratitude diary encourages you to live in the present and take stock of all the reasons you have to be happy right now.

The act of maintaining a gratitude diary is quite simple: Each day, at some point in the evening (ideally during some quiet time before you go to bed), write down several things that happened in the day for which you are thankful. You can include nice things that others did for you, things you noticed around you, and positive things you did for others.

Here is an example, using one of my gratitude diary entries:

Today I was grateful for:

- The airport security screener who complimented my smile and my eyes
- A new service offering idea I developed
- Completing another chapter of my book
- The delicious dinner I cooked for myself
- Having the time to watch a movie on my flight home from Los Angeles

As most people write the entries in their diaries, it gives them a greater sense of appreciation for their lives. Many people also talk about having a feeling of being elevated or lifted as they reflect back on their days; it simply boosts their moods. And knowing that you will be completing your gratitude diary tends to make you more aware of the many things occurring in your daily existence for which to be grateful. This process tends to work better if you write down your entries by hand as opposed to typing them on a computer or merely recounting them mentally. If you do this exercise even once a week, you will be likely to receive some benefit from it.

Interestingly, it has been found that the use of a gratitude diary can be more effective than medication or psychotherapy in treating depression.[48] Thus, an attitude of gratitude is one of the weapons that should definitely be in your arsenal for flourishing.

Reframing Negative Events

This activity can be added to your regular entries in your gratitude diary. Whenever negative events come up, your goal is to reflect on what positive can come out of them – or rather, how are they blessings in disguise? How can they help you? How might you be able to turn them to your advantage?

For example, I recall an incredibly busy month in my life when I had been burning the candle at both ends, and every time I turned around, some other meeting or obligation was being added to my work calendar. In fact, my schedule required me to be traveling much more than usual from city to city, while my consulting clients were breathing down my neck with a high level of urgency, wanting everything to be resolved immediately. Although some people thrive on running from activity to activity, I prefer to be challenged, but with adequate time to rest and recharge.

While on a trip during which I was feeling particularly overwhelmed, I took out my gratitude diary and began trying to reframe this busy time for myself. Here is what I came up with:

Negative Event: Traveling extensively with a ridiculously busy schedule

Blessings in Disguise:

- I am collecting lots of hotel points and frequent flyer miles I can use for a free vacation.
- I've met some neat people in the different cities.
- I am learning to be more efficient.
- I don't have to cook so much, since I'm never home.
- I am saving on gas by not having to commute as much.

People who have used this strategy often note that doing this activity gives them perspective and allows them to think in a more balanced way about the negative experience. They also mention that it can be a helpful means of problem solving and provides them with a sense of hope and empowerment. I recommend you experiment with it and see what sort of results you achieve.

Gratitude Visit

This exercise takes the gratitude diary experience to another level and allows you to connect with someone else in an appreciative way. To begin this activity, write down the names of two or three people who have been kind to you and whom you would like to thank. Pick one of these people, preferably one who lives close to you, and write him or her a letter expressing your gratitude for what he or she has done for you. Once you have written the letter, set up a time to meet with that person and read the letter to him or her. If you like, you can laminate it or put it on beautiful stationery so that it becomes more special. Then, leave the letter with that person.

While this may sound like a simple exercise, trust me when I say it can be an incredibly moving experience that has a positive effect on both the giver and receiver of the gratitude. For most people, even the task of writing the letter is one that gives them a sense of being lifted or a feeling of swelling in their chest. Research shows that connecting with others, as well as having friends and a sense of social support, is associated with greater happiness.[49]

You may also choose to conduct the gratitude visit with someone in your organization. This could give you more bang for your leadership buck, as it will allow you to enhance your own mood while strengthening a professional relationship. It is also a way of building stronger connections and increasing the appreciation for the positive relationships you do have.

SMILE ASSIGNMENT

Before I give you the assignment, I would like you to try a brief experiment. First, I would like for you to frown. Put on your most sullen or grouchy expression and hold it for about 10 seconds. If you are still reading but haven't actually tried this, just give it a shot – I'm going somewhere with this. Next, I would like for you to smile. Again, hold it for about 10 seconds. If you are like most people, you probably noticed a different feeling in your body when you smiled. You felt brighter, lifted, and more positive.

The simple act of activating your smiling muscles has the effect of lifting your mood. An interesting study was done in which students were asked to read cartoons while either holding a pencil in between their top lip and nose (simulating a frown, though they were not told that they were frowning) or holding it between their teeth (simulating a smile). Those in the smiling group actually rated the cartoons as being funnier.[50] Simply smiling put them in a more positive mood.

Your assignment, then, is to experiment with the effects of smiling in your own life. For a week or two, on odd days, you will make an effort to smile more than normal that day. On even days, you will smile your regular amount. Notice how things go differently for you on the days when you are smiling more.

- Do others respond to you more positively?
- Are you in a better mood?
- Is there more of a skip in your step?
- Based on this experiment, are there things you would like to do differently in your life?

In his research, Dale Jorgenson found that when you smile at people, they are more likely to smile at you.[51] The more this happens, the better your mood becomes. This makes a lot of sense on an intuitive level. When someone appears to be in a good mood, doesn't it feel better to be around them? Don't you feel more drawn to them? Try smiling more in your own life and see what type of results you get.

Savoring

Savoring refers to living fully in the moment, allowing your senses to be fully activated, and reveling in all that is going on around you. This quote from Helen Keller illuminates this idea wonderfully:

I wondered how it was possible to walk for an hour through the woods and see nothing of note. I who cannot see find hundreds of things: the delicate symmetry of a leaf, the smooth skin of a silver birch, the rough, shaggy bark of a pine. I who am blind can give one hint to those who see: use your eyes as if tomorrow you will have been stricken blind. Hear the music of voices, the songs of a bird, the mighty strains of an orchestra as if you would be stricken deaf tomorrow. Touch each object as if tomorrow your tactile sense would fail. Smell the perfume of flowers, taste with relish each morsel, as if tomorrow you could never taste or smell again. Make the most of every sense. Glory in all the facets and pleasures and beauty which the world reveals to you.

For a start, try savoring the next time you are eating a meal. Instead of chatting your way through it or shoveling it down while standing up, make your meal a feast for the senses. Create a lovely place setting at the table. Look at the beauty of the colors of the food on your plate. Take in the aroma. As you put each morsel on your tongue, feel the texture of the food. As you take your first bite, notice the sound of the crunch or the sensation of the juices spurting into your mouth. Really taste your food. For many of us, this is an entirely different experience from how we usually go about dining, and it is a wonderful reminder of how oblivious we frequently are to what is going on around us.

Try savoring other aspects of your life as well, aiming to become totally absorbed in experiences. Really listen to the beauty of the music as you are riding in your car on the way home from work. Try to notice one positive thing in each stranger as you pass him or her on the street. Appreciate the sound of the wind rustling through the trees or birds singing the next time you are outside. Luxuriate in the feel of the water against your skin as you take your morning shower. Jon Kabat-Zinn, a notable writer in the field of mindfulness, even talks about savoring the experience of washing dishes!

You can likewise bring savoring into your work environment. Aim to be totally present when you are interacting one-on-one with a colleague. Instead of being only halfway tuned in during a group meeting, really pay attention. Appreciate the strengths that each person brings to the table. Notice the unique beauty of the room in which you find yourself. As in the gratitude exercises, savoring is a way to fully appreciate the positives you have in your life. Writing about pleasant experiences in your diary or coming up with strategies to remember them (e.g., creating a scrapbook after a vacation or making notes in a journal) can help you to re-experience the activities in the future that you have savored in the past.

Acts of Kindness

Another strategy for increasing happiness is to engage in acts of kindness, as it has been found to be effective in terms of benefitting both the receiver and the giver (like a smile). As it sounds, engaging in acts of kindness simply involves doing nice things for others without any expectation of being repaid. Challenge yourself to be creative with these. Some of the favorite ones I have done include giving a friend an unexpected card just because, giving money to the unsuspecting security guard in my office tower, complimenting strangers, helping a mother or foreigner struggling through an airport, and leaving a gift on a neighbor's stoop. Experiment and I'm sure you will find performing random acts of kindness to be an excellent feel-good tool.

Lyuborminsky found that the acts-of-kindness exercises are most effective if you do them all on one chosen day of the week, as opposed to spreading them out across several days.[52] Therefore, for optimal effect, aim to do five random acts of kindness one day a week. To further enhance the benefits of this, write about your experiences in your diary so you can relive, internalize, and savor them. The result of doing this is greater happiness and sustained well-being.

Use Your Signature Character Strengths

A final strategy for increasing your level of positivity is to find opportunities to use your character strengths in your personal and professional endeavors. Psychologists Martin Seligman and Christopher Peterson described character strengths as a group of positive qualities that contribute to "the good life."[53] Historically, studying character was something from which psychologists shied away, as it was seen as value laden. However, in their work, Peterson and Seligman argued that there were certain qualities that were valued across cultures, religions, and ethnic groups.

While there may be some overlap between character strengths and the strengths you self-identified in Chapter 2, a review of their list of strengths can provide you with another lens through which to think of yourself and the unique contributions you make to the world. Read through the 24 strengths of character, broken down into six virtue categories as outlined below, and make a note of which ones resonate with you:

1. STRENGTHS OF WISDOM AND KNOWLEDGE

    a) CREATIVITY – coming up with innovative approaches to doing things
    b) CURIOSITY – having an interest in a variety of things; asking questions
    c) LOVE OF LEARNING – seeking out new information

d) OPEN-MINDEDNESS – being open to different ways of perceiving issues
   e) PERSPECTIVE – being able to keep the big picture in mind

2. STRENGTHS OF COURAGE
   a) AUTHENTICITY – being open and honest in one's presentation
   b) BRAVERY – being willing to take on challenging or daring activities
   c) PERSISTENCE – being determined and following through on tasks
   d) ZEST – enthusiasm and passion for life

3. STRENGTHS OF HUMANITY
   a) KINDNESS – being thoughtful and considerate of others
   b) LOVE – valuing connectedness and intimacy with others
   c) SOCIAL INTELLIGENCE – being empathetic and sensitive to others' needs

4. STRENGTHS OF JUSTICE
   a) FAIRNESS – having consistent principles that drive how you treat others
   b) LEADERSHIP – taking charge in leading a group toward a goal
   c) TEAMWORK – being a collaborative and supportive member of a group

5. **STRENGTHS OF TEMPERANCE**

   a) FORGIVENESS/MERCY – being compassionate and forgiving to those who have mistreated you

   b) MODESTY/HUMILITY – viewing yourself as similar to others, not better than or worse than

   c) PRUDENCE – thinking things through and using judgment in decision making

   d) SELF-REGULATION – moderating your emotions and behaviors

6. **STRENGTHS OF TRANSCENDENCE**

   a) APPRECIATION OF BEAUTY AND EXCELLENCE – being able to value beauty and outstanding achievement in a variety of domains

   b) GRATITUDE – being thankful for positive occurrences

   c) HOPE – believing in a positive future and taking steps to realize it

   d) HUMOR – having a playful and lighthearted approach to life

   e) RELIGIOUSNESS/SPIRITUALITY – having a belief about your purpose in life

To determine your top strengths, I encourage you to visit the website for the Values in Action (VIA) Strength Finder at http://www.viacharacter.org, and take a free test that will indicate your top five strengths based on your responses. Research suggests that people who engage in behaviors that allow them to leverage their strengths have a greater sense of well-being,[54] job satisfaction, and meaning in one's job.[55] In fact, in one study, employees who used four or more of their character strengths had more positive work experiences and were more likely to view their work as a calling, compared to those who used less than four.[56]

Therefore, I encourage you to find ways to use your signature character strengths as often as you can. In particular, try to mix it up in terms of how you use them. We tend to become accustomed to activities if we do them the same way every time; however, using signature strengths in a new and unique way has been shown to increase happiness.[57] Here are some examples of ways you might apply various strengths:

APPRECIATION OF BEAUTY AND EXCELLENCE

Go to a play or a sporting event. Decorate your office with items you find aesthetically appealing.

AUTHENTICITY

Strive to go through a whole day without telling any lies (even "white" lies).

CURIOSITY

Ask questions of new people you meet to learn more about them.

LOVE

Write a letter of recognition to a colleague or employee.

LOVE OF LEARNING

Read a book about something you have always found interesting but haven't previously made the time to look into. Take a course to foster your professional development.

PERSISTENCE

Set a challenging goal for yourself and work toward achieving it.

Be Consistent

> *Habits are cobwebs at first; cables at last.*
>
> —Chinese Proverb

Just as meditation is a practice that needs to be done consistently for best effect (and actually also increases positive emotions), so too is the pursuit of happiness. Thus, I encourage you to use these tools on a consistent basis. Just as you couldn't expect to stay in shape by exercising once in a blue moon, the same thing goes for maintaining an optimal level of happiness. Due to a process called kindling, we can actually change our cerebral pathways and create happier brains if we engage in these behaviors on a regular basis.

Researchers often use the analogy of an injury to describe the process of kindling. For example, I have a pesky hamstring strain on my left leg that I pretty much ignored for years. While there were times when I was "good" and rested it, stretched it, and soaked it in Epsom salts several times a week, I was often not able to resist the lure of the tennis courts or my desire to go to the gym. As such, that hamstring became prone to repeated strains, and there were times when if I even took too long a stride while walking, I strained it again.

The same process occurs with our moods. If someone is continually negative, his brain becomes skilled at acting that way, and in effect, his brain develops a habit of being in a negative, or perhaps depressed state. Thus, just like my hamstring that is prepped to strain itself in response to the most minimal of offenses, a consistently depressed person's brain will be more prone to being depressed in response to minimal triggers.

The good news is that we can train our brains (and our bodies) in the opposite direction so that they will habitually work for us in a more positive way. For example, a few years ago, I experienced a serious hamstring pull in my right leg while playing tennis. It was so bad, in fact, that I ended up going to the physical therapist, got regular ultrasound treatments, received exercises to do at home, and underwent electric stimulation of the muscles. Interestingly, even though the muscle on that leg was injured much worse than my pesky left leg, it is now the healthier of the two legs because I put more of an effort into tending to it and healing it.

You can likewise think of the happiness exercises I have provided as being "physical therapy for your brain," using them regularly to strengthen the pathways in your brain associated with happiness. In that way, you can train yourself to feel a sense of happiness in response to minimal triggers. In order for you to maintain your motivation to do them, however, you should enjoy them. Thus, experiment with the ones that seem to be the most well suited to your personality and preferences. Also, to ensure you don't become bored doing the same exercises over and over, mix it up – doing so will maintain your interest and maximize the benefits you receive from your efforts.

> *"What day is it?"*
> *"It's today,"* squeaked Piglet.
> *"My favorite day,"* said Pooh.
>
> —A.A. MILNE

PURPOSEFULLY SET A POSITIVE TONE

Now that you have a host of strategies to boost your experience of positive emotions, you can now be purposeful about setting a positive tone in your work environment.

Admittedly, if you are experiencing more positive emotion and have developed an optimistic explanation style, the tone will likely take care of itself. However, if you – like many of us – are a work in progress, then it is important to be intentional about setting the right atmosphere in your dealings with others.

If you find you have a hard time controlling your moods, you should start by working to be more self-aware. When you feel yourself descending into a negative mood, try to identify the thoughts or triggers that have contributed to it. Engage in the A-B-C-D process to try to combat any troublesome thoughts. If your negative mood persists, try to avoid emotional contagion by giving yourself some time to get yourself together, when feasible. Go for a walk, vent to a friend (if it will be helpful in lifting your mood), or take a moment to breathe or meditate. Do whatever you can to avoid negatively influencing others.

As an example, if you are chairing a meeting that will cover negative news, be purposeful about monitoring your tone. Be honest about the negative situation, but make sure to consider Churchill's quote about considering the opportunity in every difficulty. Be mindful of your nonverbal behavior – if you appear defeated, you will likely spread that attitude to those around you. Think about how you can still convey a sense of hope to your audience through the challenges. It can be helpful to practice in advance, perhaps seeking feedback from a trusted confidante. Your goal should be to balance the reality of the situation at hand with a message of inspiration, communicating a can-do spirit of confidence in the face of obstacles.

It is also important to remember the 3:1 positivity ratio in your dealings with others. Because negative emotions and experiences tend to be felt more intensely, it is important to ensure there are enough positive experiences to counteract them. Keep in mind that you are not striving to have *no* negative experiences. In addition to not being practical or realistic, research indicates that there is a point at which too much positivity becomes counter-productive.[58] For example, if employees are "ultrahappy," they may not take problems and opportunities as seriously.[59]

It can also be helpful to share the research with your employees, so they too can understand the benefits of cultivating positive emotion. Stressing to them that positive emotion will not only help them in their work lives, but also in their personal lives, can help you to gain buy-in from them to experiment with different approaches. The key, however, will be to make sure you practice what you preach. If you are espousing the importance of gratitude and kindness but behaving like the resident S.O.B., it is pretty unlikely that your employees are going to cooperate with you in aiming to create a more positive work environment. (Plus, that pesky emotional contagion phenomenon would likely make it challenging for them to be more positive anyhow!)

Research has shown that by putting the tools outlined in this chapter into practice, you will increase your likelihood of flourishing. Experiment with the various approaches and use the ones you most enjoy that fit with your personality and preferences. You will become happier, and in turn, it will enable you to become a more effective leader.

The greatest day in your life and mine is when we take total responsibility for our attitudes. That's the day we truly grow up.

—JOHN C. MAXWELL

CHAPTER SIX

AUTHENTICITY

The privilege of a lifetime is to become who you truly are.

—C.G. JUNG

I once worked with a talented and ambitious woman named Sofia who had recently been promoted to a director role in her hospital. She was a driven and determined 30-something Latina who had recently been identified as having high potential, and as a result, she had been selected to take part in a leadership development program. As the only person of Hispanic heritage in a leadership position within the organization, she was motivated to continue to grow, not only for personal reasons, but also to positively represent her family and her ethnic group.

During our work together, Sofia explained that she put a good deal of pressure on herself to come across in a way that represented her people in the most positive light. She was aware of potential negative stereotypes that others could have, so she worked hard to make sure she presented herself as conscientious, diligent, diplomatic, and professional. She was acutely observant and had excellent insights about group dynamics that she used to be chameleon-like, expertly adapting and conforming herself to best fit in with those around her.

While putting on a positive front and striving to be professional is entirely appropriate for an eager up-and-comer, the negative aspect of her focus on how she was being perceived was that Sofia did not leave herself any room to actually be herself. For example, as opposed to expressing her own opinions, she would frequently assess the tone of the group in which she found herself, and then voice perspectives she felt would be well accepted. Or, when asked about her weekends, she would be somewhat guarded, talking about activities that were the most "vanilla," but not allowing others to get to know other interesting facts about her by talking about her family or culturally-specific activities, such as when she attended her niece's *quinceañera*.

On the one hand, she expressed that she engaged in this behavior to make others comfortable. Because she felt she didn't have the same "license" to be herself as those around her, in her eyes, being vigilant about how she carried herself – and molding herself into who she believed others felt she should be – was required for continued advancement in the organization. At the same time, however, she felt conflicted about this behavior. Although she was rewarded for being non-obtrusive, she felt stifled by the need to continually conceal many of her opinions and experiences.

As a member of a minority group who has worked in corporate environments for years, I understand all too well the internal pressures that Sofia felt to be cautious about expressing her true self. And, unfortunately, I have heard this opinion commonly expressed from other members of historically disadvantaged groups, whether they be from ethnic minorities, the LGBT community, or women. Experience has taught them that they do not have the same leeway to make mistakes as their non-minority peers. While a mistake may be seen as a lapse for someone else, they fear that if they make a misstep, it will be perceived as due to a lack of ability or intelligence.

Interestingly, however, I have also heard these fears expressed by individuals who are not members of minority groups. For example, I recently worked with a white male named John who expressed that he could not be his true self in his dealings with others. As someone who was hard on himself and beat himself up for the slightest error, he assumed others viewed him in the same harsh manner. As a result, he constantly watched his "p's and q's" so as not to provide others with any additional fodder for viewing him in a negative light. In addition, when others challenged an opinion he offered, he would quickly retreat, so as not to upset his audience or create any sort of conflict.

At the core, what all of these individuals have in common is the belief that they cannot be their authentic selves in their dealings with others. They likewise share the commonality of the emotional toll it takes on them to constantly monitor themselves as they go about their work. Consistently muting *who* one is takes some effort and can create a sense that one is, on some level, betraying him or herself. However, despite their discomfort with the behavior, many clients like this have remained resolute in their belief that it is an irrefutable fact that they have to behave in such a manner to get ahead in the corporate world.

On the flip side, it is interesting to note that the colleagues of individuals who consistently manage their impressions view their coworkers somewhat differently than intended. While they are largely unaware of the degree to which their coworkers are adapting their behaviors to conform to the perceived organizational standards, they still tend to have the vague feeling that something is "off."

For example, those who shy away from conflict to ensure smooth interactions with peers may be described as intelligent, but they are less likely to be seen as thought leaders. Or, I have heard descriptions of chameleon-like individuals as being talented and skilled at getting the job done, but hard to get close to or difficult to read. As a result, they don't feel the same depth of relationship with these skillful impression managers as they might with their other more open colleagues. Somewhat ironically, by not being authentic, these individuals are actually making themselves more likely to be perceived as a member of an outgroup, as others are detecting the invisible boundaries they have erected.

To avoid this misperception, it's vital to remember that a consummate leader is one who is comfortable being her authentic self. She recognizes that her opinion may not always be popular, yet she believes that doing the right thing, being appropriately assertive, and calling out the "elephants in the room" are necessary qualities for ensuring her business makes the most effective decisions. While she uses a suitable amount of judgment and emotional intelligence in communicating her perspectives in a way that others are able to safely "hear," she is confident that having a seat at the table requires her to be an active participant in her environment.

CHAPTER SIX ⁂ AUTHENTICITY

IS IT SAFE TO BE AUTHENTIC?

No one man can, for any considerable time, wear one face to himself, and another to the multitude, without finally getting bewildered as to which is the true one.

—NATHANIEL HAWTHORNE

Over the years, I have consistently found that my clients have gained much more than they have lost by taking the risk to be more authentic. They have enjoyed greater effectiveness as leaders, enhanced confidence, and more satisfaction and fulfillment as a result of being themselves. In addition, they have experienced deeper relationships and more respect from those around them. By opening up, speaking their truth, and behaving in a way that aligns with their values, they have felt greater fluidity and comfort as leaders.

As the quote opening this section suggests, however, behaving in an authentic way isn't always as straightforward as it would intuitively seem to be. Why? Because after developing the habit of using others as the guiding force for how one should behave, some individuals find they have difficulty determining what their own beliefs are, not to mention *who* they are. If you find yourself in this category, as a first step, I would encourage you to revisit the chapters on self-awareness and purpose so you can engage in some deep reflection to understand what makes you tick. With a better awareness of your beliefs and what is important to you, you can have greater self-assurance about the value you bring to your work and how your unique perspective can inform decisions.

Another potential problem some people face is that they can become so used to self-monitoring and altering their behavior that self-censuring can become an automatic process of which they become unaware. Thus, as an additional step, I encourage you to keep track of those times during which you stifle yourself. Note them in a journal and look for themes. Are there certain topics about which you are less inclined to give your true opinions? Are there rational reasons for this? Have you seen others reprimanded for expressing their thoughts in this area? Are you being overly cautious? Strive to be as objective as possible, separating yourself from the emotions of the situation and approaching the exercise as an impartial observer. Once you have been able to go from irrational beliefs to rational, use this information to tailor how you speak up.

After engaging in this exercise, some individuals with whom I have worked have determined that their concerns are indeed well founded, and that, unfortunately, the culture of their organization is not one that is accepting of authenticity. Some observed that they were employed in a workplace that had a "good old boy" mentality in which diverse backgrounds were not valued. In others, the leaders of the organization did not support diversity of opinion, preferring instead to have a sense of artificial harmony as opposed to active debate and constructive conflict. Others simply confirmed that their beliefs or values were simply not a good fit for the organization's culture.

If you find yourself in this situation, I encourage you to engage in some soul searching. Janis Joplin once said, "Don't compromise yourself. You are all you've got." Similarly, during an inspirational commencement speech at Stanford University, Steve Jobs said:

> Your time is limited, so don't waste it living someone else's life. Don't be trapped by dogma, which is living with the results of other people's thinking. Don't let the noise of other's opinions drown out your own inner voice. And most important, have the courage to follow your heart and intuition.

Recognizing that life is finite, determine if staying in that sort of culture makes sense for you in the long term. If there is some reason that it benefits you for the present, such as getting important experience or working under an influential person in your field, then take advantage of it, but set a time limit for yourself at which point you will explore other options. Then, make a plan to find an environment in which you can be your authentic self. I have seen numerous individuals move ahead responsibly to find a suitable work environment without making rash decisions. They have maintained their effectiveness in their current settings, being careful not to burn any bridges, while seeking other opportunities that are a better fit for their values, strengths, and abilities. Once they moved past their initial fears regarding change, they transitioned into situations that provided them greater satisfaction, engagement, and fulfillment.

While there were a minority of individuals who, based on the self-monitoring exercise, decided they could not safely and authentically be themselves in their current environment, a greater number of clients determined that their beliefs about needing to censor themselves were unfounded. They may have observed others expressing opinions that they had been keeping to themselves. Usually, the other person did not experience any negative consequences, and sometimes received great acceptance or praise for her ideas. Or, they may have experimented with being assertive in an area and realized that nothing untoward happened. With a more balanced view of the situation, they reached the conclusion that they were stifling themselves based on their own fears, as opposed to an objective reality. At this point, they were ready to become more authentic and to develop as consummate leaders.

I do need to note one caveat, however. I have come across some individuals who have used the term "authenticity" as a carte blanche to engage in bad behavior. For example, I have frequently heard individuals make scathing or unkind comments and then follow them with "I'm just being honest" as a means of excusing their tactless delivery. In many cases, some of my more restrained clients view this sort of behavior as being assertive or authentic, and as a result, want nothing to do with it.

To clarify, my view of authenticity in a consummate leader is someone who can assertively state one's perspective, but in a way that is respectful, compassionate, and emotionally intelligent. After all, if you are stating your views in a way that takes others aback and causes them to react more in response to their emotional reactions than the content of what you have said, you are not being an effective communicator. Plus, as we know from the last chapter, if you express yourself in such a way that it puts others in a negative frame of mind, you are shooting yourself in the foot as a leader. Authentic communication, therefore, strikes a balance between your own needs and the needs of others.

WHO DO YOU WANT TO BE?

If you could be the sort of individual at work you would want to be, what would that look like? How would you lead others? How would you approach your work differently? To explore these questions, take a moment to consider this topic by engaging in the following exercise:

1. Close your eyes and take some deep breaths from your diaphragm. Relax your body, starting from your head and working your way down to your feet, purposefully relaxing each part of your body. Focus on

your breath for at least ten counts, aiming to separate yourself from your current stresses and to bring your awareness to your body and your breathing.

2. In your mind, fast forward one year into the future. Imagine you are embodying your best possible self as a leader at that time. Everything in your life has gone as positively as you would want it to, and you are being the leader you would like to be. For a moment, release yourself from any constraints you normally put on yourself and let yourself dream. Take some time to get a clear mental picture of yourself as your ideal self at work, and aim to truly feel what it would be like to be that person. Experience the details: What are you doing? How are you behaving? What is your physical presence like? How are you going about your work? What sorts of things are you saying? What are you accomplishing?

3. Once you have a clear picture in mind, write it down in detail, being as descriptive as possible. Use the present tense so you can identify with it fully. How does it feel? What are you like?

4. What one commitment can you make to yourself right now to move toward being this version of yourself?

Working with hundreds of senior leaders over the years, I have never come across someone whose ideal self was to be mousy, stifled, or a muted version of him or herself. Instead, people's inner desires were to fully engage their strengths, have a voice, and make an impact in their environment. Keep this version of yourself in mind as you take the next steps toward becoming more authentic.

GIVE ME AN "M!" GIVE ME AN "E!"

People who believe they cannot be their authentic selves at work tend to be quite adept at making seemingly rational arguments to convince themselves they need to be muted versions of themselves in order to succeed. Examine your beliefs in this area:

- Where did you get the idea that you cannot be yourself?
- Did you witness your parents muting themselves when you were growing up?
- Were you taught that children are to be seen and not heard?
- Did you have a negative experience with a prior boss who taught you it isn't worth it to speak up?
- Are there aspects of your cultural background that feed into your beliefs?
- Do gender roles influence your perspectives?

Explore whether your beliefs are creating a self-fulfilling prophecy. I have worked with some individuals who are so convinced that their opinions will be ignored or met with opposition that they express them so tentatively that others do not take them seriously. People respond not only to the substance of communication, but also to the way in which words are delivered. Pay attention to whether your beliefs affect how you are conveying your thoughts when you do speak up. You may unwittingly be undermining your own authority.

Now, it is time to become your own cheerleader and work to use your well-honed skills of persuasion for positive purposes. Instead of making arguments for why you shouldn't speak up or be yourself, impress upon yourself the benefits of being authentic. Think of the advantages of being true to yourself, or of being assertive in advocating for yourself. Picture the respect you will get as a result of being courageous or the higher quality relationships you will experience as a result of connecting with others on a deeper level. Make a list in your journal of all the benefits you anticipate as a result of being more authentic and review it regularly to inspire you to be more open.

Some of my clients have found it helpful to encourage themselves with quotes or biographies of individuals they admire who were authentic and had a positive impact on others. People who stayed true to themselves and achieved great success (even when it appeared they were "marching to the beat of a different drummer") indicate it can be done. There are numerous successful people in politics, business, the arts, and athletics who show the value of staying true to oneself as a means of innovating and adding value. Maintaining a list of such individuals can provide powerful inspiration to take risks and step outside of one's comfort zone in daily interactions.

In addition, I encourage you to experiment with taking baby steps toward being more authentic. Note I said *baby steps* – a gradual process can enable you to do this the most fluidly, without overwhelming others. For example, if you have been hiding by keeping your perspectives to yourself for years, then opening up the floodgates in one fell swoop may take others aback. Aim to say one thing you might not have normally said before in a meeting and see what happens. Did any of your fears come to pass? Or, were you predicting negative consequences that never actually happened? Continue to push yourself through your initial discomfort to show you deserve your seat at the table.

As you actively strive to be more authentic, persist in assessing how you feel by considering the following:

- What sort of response are you getting?
- Is your confidence increasing in your interactions with others?
- Is your nervousness decreasing?
- How are your relationships being affected?

When my clients are in organizations that they deem well suited to them, they note across the board that being more authentic has resulted in incredibly satisfying outcomes.

An additional way to achieve enhanced authenticity is to recruit a trusted colleague to provide you with feedback on how you are coming across. For example, you may sincerely believe you are pushing yourself in terms of opening up and being authentic, but others may still view you as expressing yourself in a guarded way. Conversely, as you experiment with your new behaviors, you may come across more abruptly than anticipated. Having someone coach you can help you ensure your new behaviors are perceived as intended.

Finally, recognize that being authentic as a leader can be a powerful means of setting an example for those who report to you. When individuals witness their leaders being honest and open, even with difficult topics, it encourages them to do the same. The benefit of this is that instead of having a team of people who may package what they are telling you to have the most positive effect, you can have greater confidence that you are getting the full story and won't get caught off guard by problems. At the same time, by being more open, you are modeling this behavior for those who report to you, and you can then create a safer environment for their growth and development.

To illustrate an example, I recently worked with a leader who realized that while his serious, intense, and private approach allowed him to exude a commanding presence, it also inadvertently caused him to intimidate people. To address this, he instituted a weekly meeting with his direct reports in which the topic was lessons learned from the week. Thus, as opposed to simply discussing business objectives, he created a safe environment in which his team could ask for help, be authentic, admit mistakes, and grow as leaders. He also contributed to the conversation by showing vulnerability, talking about himself, and sharing his more personal side. The meetings were a great success – many of his team members expressed it was their favorite part of the week, when they could let their guards down and bond on a human-to-human level. His willingness to open up created stronger relationships with his people and enabled him to further motivate them to produce greater results than they had previously been able to achieve.

STRIKE A POSE

When you were a child, did your mom consistently remind you to stand up straight? Research suggests she was definitely onto something in terms of helping you to become a consummate leader. While providing yourself with mental boosts and encouragement can be a helpful means of becoming more authentic, you can also take a shortcut to bolstering your confidence in the moment by being aware of your body positioning through something called "power posing."

The next time you are in a meeting, take a look around the room and observe the body language of those around you. Identify the people you perceive as having greater power and compare them to those you would identify as having less power. It is likely that the more powerful ones are taking up more room and exhibiting more expansive and open postures, whereas the less powerful ones are positioned in more constricted and closed postures. This finding is consistently found among human and non-human primates.[60,61]

An intriguing line of research, however, indicates that while these powerful and expansive postures convey power, they also *contribute* to feelings of power and physiological indicators linked with dominance. For example, in one study,[58] after having some baseline measures taken, participants were instructed to position themselves for two minutes in either a high-power pose (e.g., sitting down with feet on a desk and hands clasped behind their heads with elbows out wide) or a low-power pose (e.g., sitting with slumped shoulders and hands folded between their legs). As a result of being in this position for this short period, the high-power posers experienced increased testosterone (which is linked with dominance) and decreased cortisol (a hormone associated with stress), whereas low-power posers experienced the opposite effect. In addition, the high-power posers reported increased feelings of authority and a greater willingness to take risks than the low-power posers.

Other research has shown that not only does power posing affect the level of power you feel emotionally and physically, it also affects how others evaluate you. In another study,[62] individuals were asked to position themselves in a high- or low-power stance for two minutes, and then maintain that position as they spent five minutes preparing for a speech in which they detailed why they should be chosen for their dream job. After this preparation phase, they gave the speech.

As was the case in the other study, those who had been in the high-power positions felt more empowered than the low-power group. Afterward, when independent raters watched videotapes of the speeches, they rated the high-power group as better performers in the interview and more deserving of the job than the low-power group (without knowledge of which sort of posing the individual had engaged in before speaking). In other words, they came across as more captivating, confident, and enthusiastic during their speeches.

In addition, when the speeches were rated in terms of qualities such as how qualified, intelligent, and structured the speech was, there were no differences between the groups. In other words, although the content of the speeches was deemed to be similar, the better presentation style of the high-power posers created a more favorable reaction among the raters. Interestingly, there were also no differences found in terms of how frequently the participants engaged in high-power nonverbal behavior during the speeches. The deciding factor in how they felt and were perceived was the power posing in which they engaged *before* the speech.

The lead researcher on this study, Amy Cuddy, argued that power posing assists people in being more authentic by giving them the self-assurance and composure to let their real selves shine through. She contends that across time, the different feelings and reactions from others one gets from power posing can actually change the course of your life for the better.[63]

The great news for you is that by being aware of your nonverbal communication, you can quickly give yourself a boost that will positively affect how you feel about yourself and how others respond to you. Read on for some strategies on how to be intentional about how you use power posing and other physical strategies to assist you in being more authentic.

1. Before important interactions with others or times when you may be evaluated, take two minutes to engage in high-power poses (to avoid weirdness, I suggest you do them in private, such as in a bathroom stall or in your office). Some examples include sitting with your feet on a desk with your hands clasped behind your head and elbows out wide, standing up with your feet shoulder-width apart and your hands on your hips (like a superhero), standing up and leaning forward on a table with your hands extended, or sitting with your arm spread out on the chair next to you. The key is to take up space.

2. You can also engage in power posing while others can't see you. For example, during phone calls or when writing an important email, you can give yourself a boost by being intentional about how you are using your body.

3. Be aware of how you are positioning yourself to guard against inadvertently putting yourself in a low-power position. For example, one study found that people are more assertive after using a desktop or laptop computer than a tablet or PDA, because the computers put them in a more expansive position compared to attending to a smaller device.[64]

4. In addition to paying attention to your posture, be mindful of your tone of voice. Research has shown that people who lowered their voices in an experiment saw themselves as more powerful and were more effective at abstract thinking than those who raised their voice pitch.[65]

5. One of my favorite episodes on talk shows used to be the ones in which they would take unsuspecting

people and give them glamorous makeovers. In addition to the drama of seeing the caterpillar transform into the butterfly, one aspect I really enjoyed was seeing the makeover candidate exude greater confidence and joy as a result of the changes. Take advantage of this phenomenon by dressing in ways that make you feel good about yourself. Wear that dress you know brings out your eyes or the suit that always garners compliments. The added boost to your ego can only help you in terms of how you feel and are perceived by others.

Fake it til you become it.

—Amy Cuddy

Case Study

Lise was a leader in her mid-fifties who was being considered for promotion in her organization in response to her boss' impending retirement. Having worked for the company for the vast majority of her adult life, she was committed to the success of her area and the people with whom she worked. She was seen as a dedicated, hard worker who possessed a sunny disposition, strong work ethic, and the ability to function well as part of a team. However, as someone who was self-aware, Lise also knew that senior leaders questioned her ability to make tough decisions and assert herself in the face of conflict.

Lise acknowledged that she had earned this reputation honestly. As someone who placed a lot of emphasis on being liked and seen in a popular light, she was often quiet during meetings for fear of saying the "wrong" thing. In addition, she tended to procrastinate before dealing with interpersonal situations she anticipated might be difficult, even when she knew she needed to do something about them, because she didn't want to make others (or herself) uncomfortable. Based on her consistently agreeable and unobtrusive demeanor, she knew she would have to make some changes before she threw her hat into the ring to be considered for advancement within the organization.

The first step toward Lise's transformation was making a serious commitment to change. She felt she had a good deal of untapped potential and great ideas that were going to waste, and she recognized that her approach to work and to others had held her back. Knowing that an opportunity like this might not come up again in her career, she resolved to finally take action to step up and be the authentic leader she knew she could be.

Once she had "girded up her loins" to take action, she began to monitor the various ways she censored herself. For example, she noted that she tended to sit in the back during meetings and that her posture was not always one that indicated she should be taken seriously. So, she moved more to the front and aimed to take up more space, not in an aggressive way, but simply to take more ownership and responsibility as a leader. She found that the mere act of changing her posture gave her an immediate confidence boost that she even felt on a physical level.

Lise also noticed that she didn't express her opinions as much in meetings as she should, and that when she did, she qualified her statements and came across more tentatively than was her internal experience. To address this, she challenged herself to throw out ideas more often (labeling ideas that weren't fully formed as "brainstorms") and made sure to communicate in a more assertive manner, speaking in declarative sentences, as opposed to making statements sound like questions by raising the tone of her voice at the end of them. Immediately she noticed that her contributions seemed to be met with greater appreciation, which further emboldened her to speak up more often.

Finally, she decided to actively engage others with her sense of humor more consistently. While in her personal life she was a lighthearted individual who was known for her quick wit, she had previously decided she didn't have the same license to use her humor in the workplace. Given that her positive outlook was an important part of who she was, she decided to experiment with using her humor more consistently in the workplace. After trying it out during a few meetings with people, Lise was pleasantly surprised to discover that, as was the case in her personal life, her humor helped to lighten the mood and engage others.

A few months later, Lise assessed her transformation efforts as being a success. Not only had she received positive feedback from the CEO of her organization that he had seen her efforts to be more proactive and assertive, she also felt that in her fifties, she had finally "come into herself" as a professional. The icing on the cake was that others were so impressed with her efforts that she received the promotion she desired. And, since she was developmentally focused, like any good consummate leader she recognized that the demands of the new role would require her to step up in other ways. As such, she set new professional goals for herself and continued to grow in her new position.

> *This little light of mine, I'm gonna let it shine.*
> —HARRY DIXON LOES

CHAPTER SEVEN

POSITIVE RELATIONSHIPS

Always recognize that human individuals are ends, and do not use them as means to your end.

—IMMANUEL KANT

As part of my graduate training, I had the horrendously awful but incredibly educational experience of being videotaped while providing therapy in my psychology department's clinic. If you think that the prospect of having to watch my inexperienced self counseling others was daunting, you would be correct. However, what further multiplied my horror was the fact that I had to sit through the wretched experience of watching my videotaped sessions in front of an audience of the other fledgling psychologists who were in my supervision group. (Can you tell that I really enjoyed this experience?)

As you might expect, young psychologists focus a great deal on implementing their novice techniques during their first forays into therapy. So, during my sessions, I experimented with my newly acquired active listening skills. I said, "I see," furrowed my brow, and tried to nonverbally convey all the wisdom I had amassed in my 24 years on the planet. I tried to tolerate silences and pregnant pauses while pretending to be unaware of the video camera mounted on the wall, ruthlessly recording my every misstep to be later viewed by my colleagues.

My first supervisor, who had unlimited amounts of patience and the ability to find some nugget of goodness in even the most pitiful of our rookie attempts, consistently communicated the same message to us: the relationship is the *most* critical factor in facilitating positive change in clients. While the techniques were important, we would never be effective psychologists if we focused on interventions at the expense of building a real relationship with our clients. What we needed to do, instead of spending all our efforts focusing on using technique X or Y, was to make sure we were relating to the other person as a fellow human being with a need for connection. Interestingly, the research shows that the patient-therapist relationship carries more weight with respect to positive outcomes than factors such as specific techniques and level of experience of the therapist.[66] Relationships are the vehicle through which the work gets done.

In my work as a corporate consultant, I have seen too many leaders overlook the importance of relationships. Yes – tasks, results, and metrics are essential in the business world. But how do we best inspire people to want to dig deep inside themselves to maximize their potential and exceed their goals, as opposed to merely completing their assignments dutifully because they feel like a cog in a wheel? It is done by viewing them as whole people – individuals with hopes, dreams, motivators, and unique personal histories. By getting to really know your people (and letting them get to know you), you develop deeper bonds with them and gain a greater understanding of how to work with one person versus another to help them to fulfill their potential. Relationships create a greater sense of camaraderie that makes work more enjoyable. In turn, this creates an environment more conducive to helping people to flourish.

NO MAN IS AN ISLAND

To build relationships effectively, the key is to get to the point at which you actually *do* care about the people around you as whole people and are willing to be authentic in your dealings with them. While this may come easily to some people, for others, the prospect of doing this may cause concern. After all, many of us have been taught that work and personal life shouldn't mix. I have heard some managers argue pre-emptively that if they care too much about their people, it will interfere with their judgment if they have to make difficult personnel-related decisions. Others argue that while they might love to find out about others' families, dreams, and interests, they simply don't have the luxury to do that because of time constraints and workloads. They contend that work time should be devoted to work, and that the company is not paying them to get to know the people around them.

 Conversely, some leaders genuinely care about their colleagues and are comfortable hearing about their lives; however, they are less inclined to open up about themselves. Truly connecting with others in the workplace requires a degree of trust and self-disclosure with which they are uncomfortable. Instead of focusing on the positives that come with building deep relationships, they focus on the potential negatives in that someone could judge them or use the information they disclose against them in a harmful fashion. Instead of making themselves vulnerable, they choose to be guarded as a form of self-protection.

Vulnerability researcher, Brené Brown notes:

> Armor makes us feel stronger even when we grow weary from dragging the extra weight around. The irony is that when we're standing across from someone who is hidden or shielded by masks and armor, we feel frustrated and disconnected.[67]

These leaders would rather risk being disconnected from others than take the risk of allowing others to truly know them.

It is obvious that we can't spend all our time on the job socializing; however, contrary to the arguments I outlined above, the research and my experience as a consultant tell me that taking the time to build relationships with others in the workplace is a wise investment. For example, in Robert Cialdini's classic book, *Influence*,[68] his research indicated that people are more likely to be influenced by others they like and by whom they see as being like them.

Further research has shown that mere competence is inadequate for success at work and that being perceived as likeable plays an important role in how one is evaluated by others. In one study, highly competent individuals who were seen as unlikeable were not deemed as worthy of promotions or salary increases as those who were likeable. Interestingly, both men and women were perceived as less likeable if they achieved success in a work domain that was stereotypically associated with the opposite sex.[69]

Building strong relationships with others is an important means of finding points of commonality and enhancing connections with one another. As anyone who has been in an organization for any length of time knows, people do not simply take action as a result of hard data; "softer" subjective considerations also influence our actions. The relationships we build put us in a better position to gather important information and perspectives from others, socialize ideas, get and reciprocate help, and inspire those who report to us.

If you still find yourself unconvinced about the importance of relationships, or are convinced but find yourself uncomfortable about the prospect of having closer interactions with others, I encourage you to reflect on some of the insights you may have gained as a result of answering the questions in Chapter 2 on self-awareness. Consider the following:

1. Where did your beliefs about relationships come from?
2. How might they hold you back in life and work?
3. What benefits might you enjoy from building deeper relationships?
4. What prevents you from investing more energy into your interactions with others?

Take some time to ponder these questions, then read on for additional research that supports the importance of building relationships.

WHAT'S LOVE GOT TO DO WITH IT?

In a 1999 article that discussed the characteristics of the most productive workgroups, Gallup reported the finding that having a best friend at work was correlated with a host of positive outcomes.[70] Employees with a best friend at work were seven times more engaged than those who were not. They were also:

- 35% more likely to report their coworker was committed to quality
- 27% more likely to report that the mission of their company made them feel their job is important
- 27% more likely to report that their opinions seemed to count
- 21% more likely to report that at work, they had the opportunity to do what they do best every day

Not surprisingly, employees who have a best friend at work also report being happier in their jobs. In addition to pointing to the importance of building relationships on an individual level, these findings also stress the importance for leaders to encourage relationships amongst others in the organization, thereby creating an environment that increases the odds of people performing at their peaks. High-quality relationships at work have also been shown to be associated with having a sense of psychological safety, which in turn allows employees to engage in more learning behaviors.[71]

You may recall Barbara Fredrickson's Broaden-and-Build theory from Chapter 5, which discusses the importance of fostering positive emotions for maximum effectiveness. In addition to arguing that positive emotions broaden our perspectives and have a cumulative effect across time, in subsequent research, Dr. Fredrickson contends that the emotion that has the most powerful impact on us is love.[72]

While most of us think of love in a relatively traditional way that focuses on romance with an intimate partner or devotion to a child, she defines love in more scientific terms, calling it "positivity resonance." In a nutshell, positivity resonance occurs anytime two people share a positive emotion in person that causes their biochemistry to synchronize, while being motivated to invest in each other's well-being. So, according to her definition, positivity resonance can occur with your spouse when you say "I love you," your coworker when you share a laugh over a joke, or even the barista who sells you your coffee in the morning as you share pleasantries. Theoretically, the more frequent the experiences of positivity resonance you experience with someone, the deeper the relationship.

She argues that the research suggests that love/positivity resonance benefits us in a number of ways. For example, positivity resonance gives us a blast of oxytocin, the hormone associated with the warm, bonded feeling that mothers experience after going through labor and delivering a child. And, while the surge of oxytocin that is emitted during positivity resonance is unlikely to make you feel about your colleague the same way you do your son or daughter, it has been shown to create a deeper sense of trust between people, help them deal with pressure-packed situations, and make them more sensitive to subtle interpersonal cues. All of these factors seem to be more than simply "nice to have"; instead, they are critical to top performance in a corporate environment.

Positivity resonance also has a positive impact on emotional intelligence by regulating the efficiency with which your parasympathetic nervous system works, as measured through something called *cardiac vagal tone*. People who experience more positivity resonance have higher vagal tone, which enables them to better control their attention, emotions, and behavior – three factors that are essential for effectively interacting with coworkers.

Positivity resonance also makes you a more helpful colleague. Fredrickson's research has shown that when you are in a state of positivity resonance, you become less self-centered and more interested in others' plights. This allows you to better consider others' perspectives, which is a definite asset for effective problem solving, negotiating, and influencing in business. Positivity resonance is also associated with less of a sense of "me" and more of a sense of "we." Given the importance of good teaming to produce results, fostering love in the workplace can provide you with a competitive advantage.

Finally, positivity resonance makes you wiser – the broadened awareness that comes with it makes you better able to deal with the vicissitudes of life by giving you greater wisdom and perspective. And in addition to wisdom – which is defined by the English World Dictionary as "the ability ... to think and act utilizing knowledge, experience, understanding, common sense, and insight" – positivity resonance makes you smarter. For example, one study showed that a 10-minute pleasant conversation with someone increased subsequent performance on an IQ test.[73]

For most of us, our work lives provide us with ample opportunity to foster positivity resonance if we so choose. Being on the lookout for such opportunities not only benefits us with our own relationships, it benefits the other person as well. Think of a work environment in which the workers are wiser, better problem solvers, and more perceptive, with deeper emotional intelligence, greater trust, and higher resilience to stress. Wouldn't an organization like that have an advantage over its competitors?

The consummate leader knows that focusing on relationships and creating an environment in which connections and a collegial air exist are as important as focusing on tasks, actually helping to facilitate the accomplishment of the work at hand.

YOU CAN'T HURRY LOVE

For those of you who have now become convinced of the importance of relationship building, I have a caution for you: it cannot be approached as a "technique." I have observed individuals who embark on interacting with others as an item on their "to-do" list. They walk through the office, asking people about their weekends (although they really couldn't care less about the answers), or engaging in a bit of perfunctory small talk before getting to the business at hand. While this is a worthwhile start, it is just that: a start. Most people are pretty intuitive and can see right through this sort of behavior. Some even become offended by it, as they view it as an insincere and manipulative strategy being used to manage them more effectively.

Wharton professor, Adam Grant, who has done a great deal of research on different motives in the workplace, provides us with a framework for understanding how our approach to others in the workplace contributes to outcomes.[74] In his work, he categorizes individuals into one of three types based on how they approach their interactions with others.

Individuals from the first category – **Givers** – are generous about sharing their ideas, time, resources, and connections with others. They are genuinely interested in helping others succeed, as they see success as a resource that is plentiful, and thus do themselves no harm by helping others.

In contrast, **Takers** focus on getting the upper hand in interactions. They see success as a zero-sum game in which someone else's good fortune takes away from their potential to succeed. As a result, they have a "me first" mentality.

The third group, **Matchers** (which is the category in which most of us fall), aim for reciprocity in their dealings with others. They keep track of the ledger between giving and receiving in their relationships, and they strive to keep it as even as possible. Thus, Matchers will give, presuming the other person is equally giving; if they receive something from someone else, they feel compelled to return the favor to maintain equality.

Providing support for the idea of having caring relationships with others, Grant has found that Givers can actually achieve better outcomes in a host of areas as compared to Takers or Matchers. Paradoxically, they can also have the worst outcomes, if they allow others to take undue advantage of their kindness. However, as long as Givers guard against becoming doormats by being adequately assertive, making sure not to let their hearts rule their heads, advocating for themselves, and using their insights so they are not so unduly trusting that they don't consider others' true intents, Givers come out on top.

Why is this the case? Well, contrary to the view of many that the work world is a dog-eat-dog environment, the behavior of Takers tends to catch up with them. They may get the upper hand in the short term, but in the long run, others tend to resent their self-absorption and as a result, don't trust them. Givers, on the other hand, create a sense of good will that causes others to want to help them and to contribute to their success. Also, given that they are genuinely concerned about others, Givers have a wider and richer network than their counterparts. In turn, these strong relationships and varied connections contribute to their own success and put them in a position to better facilitate the success of others.

If a Taker or a Matcher were to focus on building relationships simply for the potential of achieving greater success, he or she would likely benefit from this activity to some extent. However, across time, others would likely catch on to what they were doing. For example, if someone noted that the quality of her relationship with a Taker was extremely one-sided, she may feel manipulated. Further, she may share this perspective with others (news can travel fast within organizations, and equally fast on the Internet), causing the results of these efforts to backfire.

While a Matcher might not have this same negative outcome (since most people are Matchers, and since he would be reciprocating others' behaviors), he would likely still not have the same extent of positive results as a Giver. The bottom line? Develop a sincere interest in others. Cultivate relationships. Even if you identify yourself as a Taker or a Matcher, focus on building relationships, but keep in mind the benefits of doing so with a giving mentality. You may find that across time, the positive reinforcement you enjoy in the form of deeper relationships changes your perspective and encourages you to build genuine connections, with the aim of assisting your colleagues. By recognizing that there is not a limited pie, but rather enough success for everyone to enjoy, you can put yourself in the appropriate mindset to build strong relationships with peers, direct reports, and others.

STRATEGIES FOR BUILDING RELATIONSHIPS

While building relationships comes naturally to some, for others, it can take more effort. Experiment with these strategies to broaden and deepen your network.

1. **Make a conscious effort to devote some time each day to relationship building.**
    For example, invite a colleague to lunch, and make sure not to spend the whole time "talking shop." Drop by someone's office and shoot the breeze. Remember the

names of your colleague's spouse and children and ask about them. While it is important to get work done in an organization, make sure you balance your results orientation with a relationship orientation.

2. **If you tend to be private, challenge yourself to be more open.**

    Keeping in mind there are obvious limits to this suggestion (i.e., your coworkers don't have a need to know all of your family drama or your deepest and darkest secrets), experiment with sharing a little more than you normally would. Strive to learn something about the other person during the conversation and to let her learn something new about you. Be a little vulnerable. When you trust others by sharing something with them, it encourages them to be more trusting of you.[75] This provides you with more opportunities to connect, as it allows them to see you as a full, authentic person with things in common.

3. **Use mindfulness in your relationships.**

    By now, based on the strong argument I made for meditation earlier in this book, you now have a regular meditation practice, right? Amongst all of its other benefits, mindfulness meditation enhances your ability to stay present with others. Listen fully to others, be respectful, minimize distractions, and employ Stephen Covey's wise adage to "seek first to understand, then to be understood." As a therapist I have learned firsthand the power of active listening. While I sometimes wish I could turn off this gift while on long flights, I have seen how being fully present with others gives them the safety to open up, which in turn deepens a sense of connection.

4. **Be upbeat and likeable.**

   While it has been said that misery loves company, research actually suggests that people who are positive are rated more likeable by others.[76] Intuitively, this makes sense. After all, who wants to spend all day with a pessimistic wet blanket? Resist the urge to get caught up in office gossip. Show your appreciation for others. Be helpful. Practice the strategies from Chapter 5 so that you become happier. All of these behaviors will cause others to feel good around you, which will make them more likely to seek you out.

5. **Be compassionate.**

   Giving others the benefit of the doubt and being compassionate when they are experiencing difficulty is another way to deepen relationships. Lest I be misunderstood, I am not suggesting that you be so compassionate that you don't address poor performance or bad behavior. What I *am* suggesting is that by genuinely caring about others, you create an environment in which positivity resonance increases, and one in which work groups feel closer. Also, when you experience greater compassion, you can address poor performance in a manner that allows the other person to receive the appropriate feedback with his or her dignity intact.

   There are a variety of strategies you can employ to become more compassionate. One strategy is a form of meditation practice called Lovingkindness Meditation (LKM), which is designed to deepen compassion by practicing being more accepting of others. Refer to Barbara Fredrickson's *Love 2.0* for an in-depth explanation of how to develop an LKM practice.

Another strategy, described by Olivia Fox-Cabane, is to imagine the person in front of you as having angel wings.[77] This encourages you to open your heart and focus on the goodness in him. It may also help you to be more upbeat, as it may be difficult to be too serious if you are imagining someone with wings!

Finally, when dealing with someone who is behaving in a difficult manner, try to look under the surface for what is causing her conduct. Is she fearful? Threatened? Embarrassed? Having an understanding of her real motives and striving to have compassion for her can help you to avoid getting drawn into her drama and enable you to behave in a positive, yet assertive fashion when responding to her. This can also help you avoid doing damage to the relationship.

If you want others to be happy, practice compassion.
If you want to be happy, practice compassion.

—Dalai Lama

Case Study

One success story that comes to mind with respect to the importance of relationships centers on someone I worked with named Douglas, an up-and-coming entrepreneurial-minded individual who had just been promoted to vice-president in his organization. Everyone recognized his talent, as he was bright, engaging, and creative. He excelled at coming up with new ideas and product lines and at finding novel channels by which to sell his company's products. However, few of his colleagues actually trusted Douglas; they described him as everything from overly ambitious and cocky to insincere and political.

When faced with feedback regarding his colleagues' perceptions, Douglas was shocked. At the core, he genuinely cared about people; however, his concern was not coming through. After some deep self-reflection, Douglas realized that his drive and focus on completing tasks actually interfered with relationships.

For example, although he had strong relationships with some people in the organization (including his boss), he realized that his deepest relationships were only with those who had some ability to further his career. And although he was someone who was friendly on the surface – frequently walking through the office, chatting up the assistants, or joking with colleagues – very often he was going through the motions, not even listening to their responses. Instead, he was thinking about the next big idea for the business or strategizing about ways to close a deal with a prospect. Thus, although he wasn't being malicious in terms of how he was interacting with people, he understood that for those who were not privy to what he was thinking, the interactions must have seemed transactional or self-serving, causing others to perceive him as a Taker.

Upon further introspection, he grasped that these behaviors played out in his personal life as well. For example, his wife frequently complained that she felt he wasn't listening to her. When faced with this complaint, he could often recite her last few sentences verbatim as evidence that he did, in fact, hear what she had said. He realized, however, that reciting sentences was a far cry from truly trying to understand her, being present, and connecting with her on a personal level.

A particularly painful realization also came when he examined how he interacted with his children. While he truly loved his kids with all his heart, he recognized that in his desire for constant achievement, he wasn't spending genuine quality time with them. Instead of giving them his full attention, he would watch TV over their shoulders, check his emails on his smartphone, or be otherwise distracted during the relatively little time they had to spend together. He recognized that things looked fine from the outside looking in, but in reality, he was unwittingly recreating the distance in the relationship he had had with his parents in his relationships with his own children.

Despite all of his accomplishments in terms of title and healthy income, Douglas felt a slight nagging hole inside of himself; even though he strived for status (and achieved it), he always felt like something was missing. He eventually came to realize that he needed to find a greater sense of balance in his life. Given his drive, he needed to continue to achieve and create; however, he recognized that he needed to deepen his relationships – both for his effectiveness as a leader and for his own personal fulfillment.

Douglas tackled this goal in a variety of ways. First, he worked to develop his listening skills by employing some behavioral strategies to reduce the likelihood he would be preoccupied during conversations. For example, if he was in the midst of something when someone dropped into his office, he told them so, and if their request was not pressing, he set up a time for them to talk or asked if he could come get them when he was finished. He also made sure to turn away from his computer screen to give people his attention. When having meetings in his office, he positioned himself with his back to his door so he wouldn't be distracted by what was going on in the hallway. Finally, if he had a great idea in the midst of a conversation, he made a quick note about it to be assured of remembering it later, as opposed to getting caught up in his thoughts while the other person was talking.

A more difficult strategy for Douglas was taking up mindfulness meditation. While he understood that part of the issue was the difficulty he had staying present with his audience, the prospect of sitting down "doing nothing" was something that brought up a lot of mixed feelings for him. Intellectually, he understood the benefits of training his mind to function in this way; yet, he doubted his ability to be able to succeed in this area. He noted that he had tried to meditate before and that he had failed miserably.

To address this, we had to ensure that he took a growth-mindset approach to meditation, understanding that it is a learned skill requiring patience to develop it. To expect that he would be able to sit down like an experienced Zen monk and contemplate quietly for an hour the first time around wasn't reasonable. So, he committed to sitting down for five minutes a day in silence, with the goal of gradually increasing it over time. This was something that seemed much more doable to him.

As he began his meditation practice, he noticed his ability to stay present in the moment improved significantly. He was less likely to have the feeling that he was missing something by focusing on the other people in his life; instead, he was able to enjoy those moments more and allow them to renew him. Once he had developed a regular meditation practice, he periodically added lovingkindness meditation to the mix. He found that focusing on others' well-being instead of his own enabled him to have greater compassion and genuine interest in them. Interestingly, it also helped him to develop greater compassion and acceptance for himself. Others felt this shift in him, further enhancing his relationship-building skills.

Douglas also made a goal of connecting with others in a more personal way. He was intentional about spending some time each day simply getting to know others and sharing aspects about himself with them. He came to enjoy and look forward to these times, viewing them as opportunities to take breaks from the hubbub of his day to recharge through sincere interpersonal connection. He found that the more he got to know others and allowed them to get to know him, the better he was able to work with them. Overall, he had an easier time influencing others because they recognized his heart was in the right place.

Across time, he genuinely moved from being a Taker who was most interested in how his interactions with others could benefit himself to a Giver who sought out opportunities to help. While he was still seen as ambitious and goal oriented, others no longer perceived him as someone who would throw them under the bus to achieve his goals. As a result, his colleagues were more likely to collaborate with him, and this further contributed to his ability to get things done in the organization.

When I ask clients to reflect on the various bosses they have had in their careers and think about the ones for whom they were willing to work the hardest, some consistent themes arise.

People were most inspired by working for positive bosses who cared about them as people and who believed in them. Yes, these bosses held them accountable, provided them with constructive criticism, and stretched them outside of their comfort zones. But there was a sense of security that came from believing that their boss understood them well enough to know what they could and couldn't handle, and that he or she would be there as a safe resource to help them dust themselves off and get back on track when inevitable mistakes occurred.

They knew that their bosses were sincerely concerned about making them better – not just for the good of the company, but for their own personal growth. Having this sort of leadership style is almost impossible without focusing on relationships. Therefore, to be a consummate leader, you must focus on building genuine connections with those around you.

> *The most important single ingredient in the formula of success is knowing how to get along with people.*
>
> —Theodore Roosevelt

CHAPTER EIGHT

COACHING AND DEVELOPING

*Management is about arranging and telling.
Leadership is about nurturing and enhancing.*

—TOM PETERS

I once worked with a manager I'll call Phil who believed in leading his employees by keeping them in a constant state of tension. At the core, Phil thought that if employees became too comfortable, they would become complacent. As a result, he frequently led through fear and exceptionally high standards. Although he had the capacity to be quite charming at times, employees were never quite sure when he might have an outburst or an excessively critical reaction in response to a mistake, and as such, his goal of keeping them off-kilter was a success.

When he provided positive feedback, Phil was reluctant to provide too many accolades, because he believed that employees who know they are doing well are less motivated to work hard. So, it was not uncommon for his people to walk away from meetings – in which they expected to be celebrated for their accomplishment – in a state of disenchantment for the nitpicking that followed the "attaboy." Even his high performers who had never personally experienced strong criticism from him frequently felt they had to walk on eggshells as a result of observing attacks on one of their colleagues. Amazingly, Phil could never understand why, even when he was in good spirits, his people eyed him suspiciously, waiting for the next shoe to drop as opposed to actually enjoying the jovial interaction.

As you might imagine, Phil's area experienced a great deal of turnover, as many people were simply unwilling to work under such an oppressive and unrewarding regime. Yet, despite the fact that young and talented employees left in droves, he convinced himself that his leadership approach was effective, as the people who stayed generally achieved the goals and metrics he set for them. What he did not know, however, was the extent to which many of the employees were working with a great deal of resentment, consistently plotting their escapes and contributing to a negative organizational culture through constant complaining about his antics. Unfortunately, this negativity created a lot of unnecessary buzz and swirl that frequently got in the way of getting the work done.

If you've been in the work world for any length of time, I'm sure you have also come across individuals who have some similarities to Phil. These people are much more focused on results than relationships – as long as the goals are attained, they aren't concerned about the process by which they are achieved. Consequently, they tend to push or pull people toward achieving goals, rather than inspiring them to grow and become the best they can be. And while these managers may be able to produce the desired results for the organization, they do so at a cost, as their people's morale is usually negatively affected. Also, what they fail to realize is that the research shows they would be able to achieve even more outstanding outcomes if they placed more emphasis on creating a positive environment for their employees.

While Phil is a somewhat extreme case, I have come across similar leaders who, like him, place an inadequate focus on interpersonal factors at work, unaware of the cost of doing so. Some of these individuals believe that people are paid to work and to do the tasks assigned to them, and therefore they shouldn't have to worry about how their people feel. Others lament that they wish they had the luxury of developing their people or connecting with them but don't have the time to do so. Still others are simply uncomfortable dealing with intangible "soft" issues, and as a result choose not to address them. Unfortunately, what all of these leaders overlook is that taking the time to coach their people and address their needs would save them a good deal of time in the long run, as they would have a more effective team supporting them.

In his book, *The Advantage*, management consultant and author Patrick Lencioni differentiates between smart organizations and healthy ones.[78] A smart organization (or leader) is one who focuses on the "traditional" aspects of business, such as strategy, finance, technology, and marketing. These leaders believe that by having the correct business strategy, processes, and objectives, along with the smartest people, they will achieve the best outcomes.

On the other hand, leaders who address organizational health are more inclined to focus on morale, productivity, minimizing politics, and fostering collaboration. They recognize that even with the best strategy, if people are not able to work together effectively and develop their talents, the interpersonal issues will impede their ability to execute. As such, they focus on issues like trust, communication, teamwork, accountability, and encouraging people to act in the best interests of the organization's goals as opposed to their own area's individual goals.

In an ideal situation, a leader should address both smarts and health in her work; however, Lencioni argues that if the focus could only be on one, health trumps smarts. He contends that leaders who focus on *how* the work gets done give their organizations a competitive advantage, since many of their competitors do not attend to these "softer," harder-to-measure considerations. And when a team works together effectively, the whole is frequently greater than the sum of its parts.

A consummate leader knows that to be most effective, his employees need to maximize their potential. He could have the best strategy on paper, but if his people are not able to attain it, it will not bear fruit. Thus, to help his people to develop, he needs to assess them as individuals, look for the best in them, leverage their strengths, and encourage them to grow. The better they are performing and the more engaged they are, the more he is able to focus on high-impact activities, while his employees shine in their individual roles.

A consummate leader realizes that people are more loyal and motivated when others take an interest in them and are concerned with their overall well-being. By fostering a developmental culture, he creates an environment in which everyone can set goals, experiment with new behaviors, and continuously improve across time.

Consummate leaders also take pride in seeing the people who report to them advance into other roles. Instead of wanting to hoard their talents for themselves, they recognize that their organizations are best able to prosper when talented people are able to grow and deploy their skills and abilities for the best interests of the organization, in whatever capacity best suits their professional development and the company's goals. They also know that employees with high morale are better employees who are more likely to help their colleagues, provide quality customer service, and persist through difficulties.

WHERE ARE YOU GOING?

Back in graduate school when I was learning to become a psychologist, it sometimes amazed me how during our sessions together, clients would frequently say something like, "Remember what you told me two months ago about topic x?" Given the number of people I saw, I frequently had no recollection of the supposed pearl of wisdom I had bestowed upon them (though I never actually admitted it). At that point in my career, I found it hard to believe that clients might go off after the session, pondering things that "little old me" might have simply said in passing. It took me a while to understand the amount of influence I had in people's lives and become comfortable with that degree of power, as well as more intentional about consciously using that influence to effect positive change.

While there are some leaders who revel in their ability to influence outcomes in people's lives, many others are more like my graduate-school self. They are unwittingly unaware of the degree of impact they have in some cases, or in other cases are in denial about the effects their behavior can have on those who report to them and the work they produce. While it might seem a bit daunting to a new leader to recognize the power she can wield in shaping her people and the results of her area, it can also be seen as a great opportunity.

Individuals who willingly and responsibly take on the mantle of leadership can not only guide the people with whom they work, they can shape families, communities, and the world. While most of us may not have the influence of someone like Martin Luther King, Winston Churchill, Susan B. Anthony, or Joan of Arc, individuals like that are excellent reminders of the impact leaders can make in transforming others, by inspiring them to see the best in themselves and successfully go after seemingly unattainable goals.

To become an effective leader, it is important to have a clear vision of the sort of mentor and guide you aspire to be. In Chapter 6 on authenticity, I took you through a visualization exercise in which I asked you to fast forward one year in the future to picture your ideal self. The emphasis of that exercise was to get you more in touch with how you would like to present yourself at work on an individual level. Now, I would like you to reflect on the sort of leader you would like to be by working through the following exercise:

1. Get your journal or a piece of paper and write down the names of some leaders you admire. Some may be former (or current) bosses who were particularly inspirational to you or who helped to get the best out of you. Others may be colleagues or people in your organization you perceive as being good leaders. Perhaps there is someone in your church or another community organization of which you are a part whom you think is particularly effective at leading people. Are there any famous figures whose leadership styles you respect?

2. Beside each person's name, list the characteristics you admire. Consider the following questions, and jot down your ideas:

(a) How do they interact with the people they lead?

(b) How do they conduct themselves?

(c) What sort of values do they possess and convey to others?

(d) Why are they so effective?

(e) What are their strengths?

3. Keeping in mind that you are an individual and will have your own unique style, are there aspects of their leadership styles you would like to emulate? Do they give you any ideas about qualities in yourself you could develop to enhance your leadership skills?

4. Think about yourself when you have been particularly effective as a leader. What were you doing and how were you being?

CHANNEL YOUR INNER CHER HOROWITZ

As we learned in Chapter 5, the importance of creating a positive and developmentally oriented environment for employees cannot be overstated. Without a safe environment in which people feel they have the opportunity to make (well-meaning) mistakes from which they can learn, innovation is unlikely to occur. Without an optimistic culture that is focused on abundance, opportunity, and growth, people are unlikely to be inspired. Without a manager who emphasizes personal development, employees are unlikely to reach their full potentials.

Consummate leaders understand that while having a talented staff increases the odds for great results, their approach to leadership plays a critical role in getting the absolute best out of their people. As noted earlier, leaders have a disproportionate amount of influence on the mood of those around them. In addition, the beliefs about their people's ability to achieve can actually affect the results they are able to achieve.[79]

This idea was illustrated in the 1995 comedy, *Clueless*, starring Alicia Silverstone and Brittany Murphy. In the film, Silverstone's character, Cher Horowitz, took Murphy's Tai Frasier under her wing to help her to become more popular. After providing her with a makeover and putting in time and effort to teach her the tricks of the trade to gain acceptance from her classmates, Cher was indeed successful in increasing Tai's status at school. In fact, much to Cher's chagrin, Tai actually surpassed her in popularity.

While Cher definitely had her flaws, she was clearly a skilled coach and mentor of Tai. She saw a glimmer of something in her that she nurtured to help the "tragically unhip" Tai become more than she ever would have envisioned for herself. And although Cher didn't appreciate Tai's popularity when it exceeded her own, she did achieve the goal that a consummate leader should strive for: *to develop her people to the extent that they could succeed her in her role.*

Cher's approach exemplifies the Pygmalion effect, named after the play by George Bernard Shaw, which refers to the finding that others frequently live up to our expectations of them. Just as Eliza Doolittle went from a girl with a strong Cockney accent selling flowers on the street to a genteel society lady under the guidance of Professor Henry Higgins, so too have studies shown that individuals are more likely to blossom when coached by others who believe in them.

For example, in the classic "Pygmalion" study conducted in the 60s, Rosenthal and Jacobsen randomly selected some elementary school students and identified them to their teachers as being gifted.[80] Although the students were no more talented than their peers (because they had been randomly assigned to that group), they eventually did exhibit enhanced performance, based on their teachers' expectations. The researchers hypothesized that because the teachers expected the children to prosper, they instructed them differently than their peers, perhaps giving them more encouragement, feedback, and patience, while also giving them stretch opportunities in the course of learning.

A similar effect was reported in a work setting by Eden in his research with the Israeli Defense Forces.[81] Again, he found that individuals who were expected to achieve high performance levels (despite the fact that their assignment to "high performer" category was entirely at random), did indeed outperform their peers. Upon further analysis, it was seen that their platoon leaders tended to look upon the "high-potential" soldiers' mistakes as opportunities for teaching as opposed to a reflection of their lack of ability. This increased the soldiers' levels of confidence, enabling them to have greater expectations of and belief in themselves.

In a nutshell, the leaders in these studies took more time and attention in grooming those they believed were capable of high performance. Not surprisingly, the individuals who had been identified as having high potential also rated their leaders more favorably than did their peers because the leaders were, in fact, conducting themselves differently with them.

Conversely, Eden describes the Golem effect, which is the opposite of the Pygmalion effect. In this phenomenon, low expectations are seen to have a negative effect on performance. While this has not been studied as much due to ethical considerations, there has been evidence of this trend in classroom studies.[82] It makes intuitive sense that if a leader doesn't expect much of someone who reports to her, she is unlikely to want to invest as much time, energy, and money into that person's development as she would toward someone she sees as more capable.

Therefore, as a leader, it is critical to do an honest self-evaluation to get a sense of your attitudes about people and those who report to you. You need to be able to catch yourself when you set the bar too low, or when you put inadequate attention into developing your people. Conversely, you need to see the spark of talent in all of the people who report to you, so you can cultivate it and help them to grow. To assist you in developing a greater sense of self-awareness in this area, reflect on the following questions:

1. How much time do I put into coaching and developing others? Do I make it a priority? Why or why not?

2. What expectations do I have of others? Do I expect people to come to work wanting to perform and achieve? Or do I see others as having to be closely watched and "managed" to be able to perform?

3. How do my beliefs affect how I lead others? How might my behaviors influence the beliefs others may develop about themselves and their abilities to perform in their roles?

4. Are there any systematic biases in terms of the expectations I have of others? Do I have any prejudices related to sex, race, age, sexual orientation, personality type, etc.? How might these influence my approach to leadership with different people?

5. What sort of expectations do I set for others? Do I provide stretch goals and coaching to help individuals achieve them? How do I engage people and let them know I care about them, their performance, and career progression?

6. How do I respond when others make mistakes? Do I create an environment that is conducive to learning? How open am I when others ask for help?
7. Do my words and actions build confidence in my employees and encourage them to believe in themselves? Why or why not?
8. Do I have any employees for which my expectations are low? How does this affect that individual and the functioning of my area? What can I do about this situation? Do I need to provide this individual with additional training, feedback, and support? Is this person simply not well suited to the role? Would he/she be better served pursuing another job that is a better fit for him/her?
9. Am I threatened at all by my people? Is there any part of me that doesn't want to develop them so I can maintain my own feelings of competence?
10. Given my answers to the previous questions, what commitment can I make to improve my ability to coach and develop people?

Take your time answering these questions, and try to think of specific examples to guard against idealizing yourself as a leader. Seek feedback from trusted others to ensure their perceptions are aligned with your own.

GETTING TO KNOW YOU

In my discussions with people about what they most desire in a boss, I consistently hear the message that workers value working for someone from whom they can learn, especially one who takes an interest in them as a person. They feel most loyal to leaders who take the time to discuss their careers with them, so they can make smart choices and reach their professional goals.

Interestingly, these self-reports align with recent neuroscience research. In one study, participants were asked to think about past experiences with resonant leaders, meaning those who are emotionally intelligent, empathetic, skilled at building connections, and focused on creating a harmonious work team.[83] When reflecting on these experiences, areas of the brain associated with aroused attention, the social network, and positive relationships were activated.

Conversely, when they thought about dissonant leaders – or leaders who are more authoritative and aim for greater social and emotional distance from employees – participants showed a different physiological profile. In those instances, the portions of the brain associated with social aspects were deactivated, while parts of the brain associated with narrowed attention, decreased compassion, and negative emotion were activated.

In another study, it was found that when individuals are coached in a compassionate way, their brains respond in ways better suited to learning.[84] In this instance, college students were given two coaching sessions. In one session, a positive approach was taken in which they were asked about their future dreams and aspirations (e.g., "If everything worked out ideally in your life, what would you be doing in 10 years?"). In the second, more negative session, the students were asked about their performance compared to ideal standards (e.g., "How are you doing with your courses? Are you doing all of the homework and readings?").

Brain scans showed that in the positive coaching session, parts of the brain associated with visual processing, seeing the big picture, empathy, emotional safety, and motivation were activated. In other words, the portions of the brain that indicated they felt secure enough to open up and were motivated to pursue goals were activated. By contrast, the negative coaching session activated regions of the brain associated with self-consciousness and feelings of guilt. Richard Boyatzis, a professor of organizational behavior argues:

> the neuroscience findings emerging suggest a basic reason why inspiring and supportive relationships are important – they help activate openness to new ideas and a more social orientation to others.[85]

Yet, often when I sit with leaders, there is a disconnect between what employees want from the leader and the sort of coaching they are receiving. Many have not had discussions with their direct reports about their career goals, and as a result cannot clearly articulate their aspirations. Therefore, they are unable to provide them with targeted advice or help them to be purposeful about taking steps to accomplish their objectives in the most effective manner.

Still, in my conversations with leaders, I find that their intentions are usually good. Most of them do care about the people who report to them; however, in endeavoring to fulfill the many demands placed upon them, they get caught up in their day-to-day responsibilities and do not take the time for these important conversations. As such, their one-on-one meetings frequently have more in common with the "negative" approach, in which they check in regarding the employee's ability to keep up with their to-do list as opposed to tapping into their aspirations and larger professional goals.

To be a consummate leader, you have to make developmental discussions a priority. Taking the time to connect with people and help them grow not only helps to build your relationship with them, but it also can be an important motivational tool. When they know that the work they are doing today connects with their goals for tomorrow, it provides them with an additional burst of energy to push themselves when the going gets hard. In addition, the more effective your people are in their jobs, the more effective your area becomes; the better your people are, the more you can delegate to them, thus freeing you up to work on high-priority activities. Not taking the time to have these conversations is a short-sighted approach that may save you some time in the immediate future, but will increasingly work against you in the long run.

So, in the midst of dealing with the many requirements on your plate as a leader and the stresses of accomplishing your targets and meeting deadlines, how do you attend to professional development?

First, I recommend having career conversations with your direct reports twice a year or so. Performance evaluations provide a natural time for having such conversations; however, I also suggest having them at the halfway point in your year to check in, see how people are feeling in progressing toward their goals, and fine-tuning as need be. Ask them where they see themselves next year at this time, five years from now, and where they would ultimately like to be.

While some people have clear ideas about the position they would like to attain, others take a more open-ended approach (e.g., "I want to be challenged." Or "Position isn't really important to me, but I want to have an impact."). If you see something in the individual that he may or may not see in himself, sharing your perspective can be very helpful, perhaps inspiring him to take on greater roles. Conversely, if you see the person's goal as unrealistic given where he is right now or how he is currently performing, it is important to give respectful feedback. Perhaps he needs to give himself more time, or address blind spots of which he is unaware. The goal of this discussion is not necessarily to change the person's mind, but to have an accurate gauge of where he wants to go so you can help him in the most effective manner.

Once you have a sense of the person's goals, brainstorm with her about the sorts of experiences that would benefit her. Is there a project she could work on? Does she need to return to school to get more education? Would an informational interview with someone in the field help her? Do you have anyone you could connect her with to mentor her? Be as specific as possible, and agree upon timelines during which the individual will pursue these action steps.

During your regular one-on-ones with your direct reports, set aside a portion of at least one meeting per month to have developmental conversations. While some leaders are very intuitive about how to have these conversations, others can struggle. Thus, here are some tips you can use in your discussions with your people:

1. Encourage them to reflect on the self-awareness questions earlier in the book and/or to go through some sort of personality assessment. Assure them that you aren't expecting them to share all of the details of their family history, but that it can be helpful for them to share any insights they might have gained that are work related. Ask them for their perceptions of their strengths and developmental opportunities.

2. Talk about how your perceptions align with theirs. Given the demands of their current role and their future aspirations, discuss how they can be more intentional about leveraging their strengths to their

advantage. While a lot of people tend to focus on their weaknesses in developmental conversations, emphasize the importance of being aware of their positive qualities, as leveraging a strength is a relatively easy way to make a big impact in one's career.

3. Pick one or two developmental areas on which they can work and develop targeted action plans to work on these areas. Write them down and check back on them consistently to provide external accountability. Commit to giving them ongoing feedback about how they are doing, and let them know that some time will be spent monthly talking about their progress and fine-tuning their plans as needed.

4. Share your own developmental opportunities with them. This creates a culture that normalizes professional development and stresses the importance of getting help from others.

5. Incorporate others into the plan as is appropriate. Encourage them to learn from their peers or other individuals in the organization who may be strong in the areas in which they could stand to develop.

6. Be consistent! Your direct reports will be able to pick up from you how much emphasis you put on development by how consistent you are in following up on it. Too many leaders have perfunctory conversations once a year, inadvertently demonstrating to their people that professional growth is not a priority. In nurturing their development by having in-depth conversations on a monthly basis, not only will you show your commitment to them, you will hone your skills as a consummate leader.

CHAPTER EIGHT ❧ COACHING AND DEVELOPING

> *I've learned that people will forget what you said, people will forget what you did, but people will never forget how you made them feel.*
>
> —MAYA ANGELOU

THE OTHER F-WORD

No, it's not the f-word you're thinking of – the one that I was assaulted with 506 times during my recent outing to see *The Wolf of Wall Street*. It's the other f-bomb that causes so many leaders to scurry into their offices, develop involuntary ticks, and be overwhelmed with a feeling of dread. What's the word? Feedback.

Although most people crave feedback and want to know how they are performing, those same people are sometimes not very effective in providing it to others. Some leaders wait until they are forced to give feedback during annual evaluations and either hit people between the eyes with constructive criticism they haven't heard all year, or else gloss over any areas for development by giving their people all 5's (on a scale of 1–5), indicating that they must be absolutely perfect in every way.

I have witnessed some leaders who err on the side of providing so much negative feedback that their people feel they can do nothing right. Some of these leaders take a Simon Cowell approach in which they say "I'm just being honest" as they rip the person to shreds. On the other hand, some leaders inadvertently hold their people back with the well-meaning, but generally unhelpful "Keep doing what you're doing!" There are also the "no news is good news" types who provide little to no feedback at all. Finally, there is a small group of individuals who are able to give feedback effectively, honestly, and respectfully. Whether you are a Simon Cowell, Paula Abdul, or Randy Jackson in your approach to giving feedback, you have the capacity to get better at shaping others' development.

Across the years, it has been my experience that a large number of leaders dread providing others with constructive criticism. Perhaps they grew up with the message, "If you can't say something nice, don't say it at all," or they may worry about how the other person will react when they provide him with suggestions for improvement. Thus, for many people, I have found it necessary to reframe how they think of feedback.

I come from a musical family, and when I was four years old, in response to my incessant begging, my mother sat me down at the piano and commenced my lessons. At the age of seven, with the highly regarded piece, "Three Blind Mice," I auditioned and was taken on as a student by my wonderful teacher, Mrs. Vera Shean. For the next nine years, until I graduated from high school, I was trained as a classical pianist under her tutelage. While I would be lying if I said I always enjoyed getting up early to practice before heading to school, looking back, the lessons were a great experience for me in terms of recognizing the value of regular feedback.

As a classical musician, it was a basic assumption that there was no such thing as a perfect performance. So, every week, I went in with the expectation that I would be getting lots of feedback. At each lesson, I would play my assigned pieces, and Mrs. Shean would compliment me for the progress I had made, or call me out when I clearly hadn't practiced enough (this was a regular occurrence when it came to scales). Then, she would help me to fine-tune in different areas. Perhaps I was rushing one piece or not playing expressively enough in another. Perhaps I needed an exercise to play a difficult section more evenly or to exaggerate the volume in my left hand to ensure the audience could actually hear the melody. Each week, my manuscripts were the recipients of more and more pencil markings, and the assignment book that I dutifully brought was filled with notes to remind me of the areas on which I should be focusing during my practice. I never resented her feedback because I expected it, knew she had my best interests at heart, and recognized that the purpose was to help me to be my best as a pianist.

Over time, techniques that were originally difficult became easy. For example, while my initial attempts at playing staccatos in my right hand while playing legato in my left were clunky and labored, eventually I was able to perform this feat effortlessly. Did Mrs. Shean ever feel guilty for giving me feedback? Given that she provided it in such copious amounts, I truly doubt it! She recognized my potential, wanted to cultivate it, and as a result, saw it as her responsibility to encourage me while pointing out areas in which I could grow. If she had chosen instead to tell me that everything was great when it wasn't because she didn't want to hurt my feelings, I never would have become as accomplished as I had been, winning various music competitions.

When I tell leaders about my experiences with Mrs. Shean, they immediately get it. Perhaps they hearken back to learning a sport, and the role their coach had in helping them adjust their backhand or clean up a jump-shot. Or, they think about the math teacher who took the time to help them to understand calculus. With those experiences in mind, they see feedback in a non-threatening way, as helpful information designed to help someone improve. Also, as they think of their roles as leaders, they realize that providing feedback is not something that is merely nice to have, it is a necessary responsibility.

Still, while being willing to communicate feedback is crucial for being an adept coach and developer, it is also a skill that requires practice and attention to perform it effectively. If Mrs. Shean had been one of those teachers of yore who had rapped my knuckles with a ruler every time I hit a wrong note, I can guarantee I wouldn't have progressed as I had. If she hadn't set the bar high, deciding "good enough" was okay when I was capable of better, I wouldn't have grown. Conversely, if she had expected me to play the "Pathétique Sonata" when I was eight, I wouldn't have had much success due to feeling overwhelmed and frustrated. Expecting the best from those you lead, while meeting them where they are, is an important part of being a strong leader. Read below for some helpful strategies to provide effective feedback.

1. Feedback is best given when the person receiving it understands that you have his best interests at heart. Thus, focus on building relationships with your direct reports so they appreciate that you are interested in them as whole people, not simply as people who work for you. Relationships create a healthy foundation for feedback.

2. Make sure you are in the right frame of mind when providing feedback. Do a self-check to ensure that you truly want to give feedback to help the person to improve. Unless they engaged in egregious behavior and you need to let them know the impact of their actions, giving feedback when you are angry is rarely constructive.

3. Aim to give feedback in a timely manner. The closer the proximity to the behavior in question, the more the individual can remember what she did well, or how what she did may not have come across as intended.

4. Be sensitive to timing. For example, if someone is stressed out because he just blew a presentation, is dealing with a dying parent, or having car troubles, you may not want to provide lots of coaching on the finer points of public speaking, for example, as he may not be in the right frame of mind to be able to process the feedback you are providing. If, however, you are checking in with regard to how he is doing and ensuring he is tending to his stress appropriately, the timing would be right.

5. There is a general adage that you should provide corrective feedback in private. Unless you have a highly functioning team that consistently provides colleagues with feedback, it is usually best to take the person to the side when giving him or her some pointers for improvement. Many people appreciate receiving recognition in front of others, so giving positive feedback or thanks during group meetings or via email can be reinforcing for various people.

6. Give the person a heads-up so that she can mentally prepare for receiving feedback. You might ask for permission to give her feedback or say something like, "I wanted to give you a bit of coaching. Is this a good time to talk?" While unlikely, if the person never asserts it is a good time to talk, you will obviously need to provide the feedback anyhow.

7. Like Mrs. Shean, look for opportunities to give positive reinforcement and corrective feedback. While "sandwiching" negative feedback between positive statements is a strategy a lot of people employ, I have found that at times, the corrective feedback can get lost in the shuffle, causing the person

to lose out on a potentially valuable opportunity to improve. Still, for most people, the bulk of your feedback should be positive and encouraging (keep the 3:1 positivity ratio in mind).

8. Make sure you are clear when providing feedback. I have sometimes witnessed leaders who were so vague, or who have sugar-coated feedback so much, that it was obvious the other person didn't realize she was actually receiving corrective feedback. By the time you have finished sharing your comments, the person should have an accurate assessment of how she is performing.

9. Be as specific as possible, noting observable behaviors. For example, if someone's averted eyes cause him to appear less confident, let him know. Or if someone's use of humor helped to engage an audience, reinforce her efforts.

10. Show confidence in the other person. Even if he is not performing well, discuss ways he can improve. Think of constructive feedback as problem solving. When providing someone with feedback, I like to envision myself working side by side with him to figure out how to address the behavior in question.

11. Remember the importance of instilling a growth mindset in those who work for you. Reinforce effort as well as results, and communicate your belief that they can learn the skill in question. Think of shaping, a technique used to train animals (and humans), in which successive approximations of a behavior are reinforced. For example, to train a rat to press a lever, at first it might be given a pellet of food for turning its head in the direction of the lever. Then, the

reinforcement might come for taking a step toward the lever. Various other behaviors are rewarded until it finally learns to press the lever. As someone is learning a new skill, reinforcing progress is an important learning and motivational tool.

12. Avoid evaluative judgments when giving feedback. Instead of making assumptions about the other person's motivations, keep the feedback focused on her behavior and the direct impact of it. For example, instead of saying, "You were disengaged in the meeting," you could say, "When you were on your smartphone in the meeting, it made you look as if you were disinterested."

13. Note the person's reaction when you are providing feedback. If she gets upset, it does not mean you should refrain from providing her with feedback; however, it can be helpful to check in with her. You might empathetically note, "I notice you seem to be getting upset. Can we talk about that?" Underscore that no one is perfect and that you are giving feedback to help her to grow.

14. Recognize that for some people, feedback can be hard to hear. Still, like a good coach, that should not be a deterrent from providing it. Make sure to articulate your feedback clearly and focus on how to solve the problem.

15. If the other person becomes defensive, note it. You could say something like, "It seems that you might not fully agree with what I'm saying. I ask that you hear me out so you can get my perspective." Encourage him to go think about it and to seek some feedback from others.

16. Recognize that even if you give feedback well, you cannot force others to accept it or to change their behavior in response to it. However, you will know that you have done your duty as a leader.

17. Be willing to ask for feedback yourself and model being open to receiving it. This helps to create a developmental environment.

18. Practice! I have found many people who initially balked and experienced cold shakes at the prospect of giving others corrective feedback became comfortable and effective coaches with enough repetition and practice.

In sum, to be sure you are placing enough time and attention on nurturing the talents of those under your leadership, you should be having developmental conversations on a regular basis. Yes, some development will require time outside of work, such as educating oneself on a topic or attending a seminar. However, given that the issues on which they will be focusing are work related, there will be ample opportunity to get on-the-job training and practice, whether it is experimenting with different influencing behaviors, structuring and organizing themselves more effectively, delegating appropriately, or the like. Being an adept developer of talent is what separates a true leader from an individual contributor, and as such, is a skill a consummate leader cannot overlook.

A coach is someone who can give correction without causing resentment.

—JOHN WOODEN

CHAPTER EIGHT / COACHING AND DEVELOPING

ONE SIZE DOESN'T FIT ALL

The final point to keep in mind when coaching and developing others is that one size does not fit all. As a leader, it is your job to determine not only the unique strengths and developmental opportunities of each member of your team, but also the ways to best motivate them. While most people respond well to positive reinforcement, what is reinforcing to them will vary.

For example, although I noted previously that there is the general rule of thumb to recognize others' accomplishments in public, I have met some people who are mortified to receive recognition in front of an audience. Further, while one person may be driven by money, another may be motivated by the opportunity to engage in meaningful work that touches others. You will know that you understand your people adequately when you can clearly articulate their goals, motivators, and what brings meaning to them.

In addition, your approach will vary depending on the needs of each person in question and his or her work style. For example, while one person may be able to work autonomously after being given a general goal, another may require more structure and check ins. They could both be valuable members on the team who bring different strengths to the organization; however, to get the most out of them, you will have to lead them differently. While the foundation of who you are as a leader will remain constant, being able to flex as needed will enable you to get the most out of the greatest number of people.

Case Study

I once worked with an individual named Amanda, an up-and-coming executive who had joined the organization five months prior to our meeting. Amanda had all the makings of a consummate leader – she was bright, upbeat, driven, and self-aware. She was a transparent communicator who excelled at building relationships and creating a sense of excitement amongst those who reported to her. Her experience with a variety of other companies gave her a varied perspective that she used to bring fresh ideas to her area. Given that she was a perpetual student who had a keen interest in her own self-development, she was a lot of fun for me to work with as a coach.

As we talked through her opportunities for development, we targeted a need for her to become an even more effective developer of people. Amanda recognized that although she was skilled at inspiring people, she had some opportunity to hone her ability to provide others with feedback. She realized her sunny disposition was both a strength and an opportunity – while it enabled her to create an upbeat environment, it sometimes made her blind to the developmental needs of her people. Thus, her goal was to become a more discerning coach.

To start, she had conversations with all of her people to determine their career goals and to get a sense of opportunities for development. The discussions were very reinforcing to her, as she discovered that in the five short months she had been there, her natural curiosity and compassion had resulted in her already having a pretty good awareness of her people's aspirations, motivators, and strengths. She realized, however, that she had a more difficult time determining areas in which they could develop. And though she had been in the organization only a short time, she knew she could not use it as an excuse, as she had similar issues in previous settings.

She found that the conversations she had with her direct reports gave her some ideas about areas on which they could work; however, she also decided to set a different standard when observing them. As opposed to only thinking about how they were performing in their current roles, she thought about what each person would need to do to achieve his or her future career objectives. She channeled her favorite coach, Mike Kryzewski, thinking about how he shaped his players by expecting a lot of them and by giving them the information they needed to improve. With this framework and a higher bar in mind, she was able to identify developmental targets for each of her people and collaboratively create action plans to achieve them.

As part of her discussions, Amanda also asked her people for feedback. Because of her temperament and the strong relationships she had built with each of them, they were very forthcoming. Based on their input, she determined that while her energy was infectious, it also caused her to move too rapidly, making it difficult for others to keep up with her. Because she was so smart, she was a quick study; however, she unwittingly expected others to process information at her same rate. She was mortified to find that, despite her good intentions, she was not as good a teacher as she had thought. Because things came easily to her, others assumed they should learn just as quickly. Thus, they were embarrassed about asking questions or requesting she should slow down. This was a critical insight for her – she had taken her intellect for granted. Having a greater awareness of this skill enabled her to stop overplaying it into a liability.

By slowing herself down and making a concerted effort to be on the lookout for opportunities to provide constructive feedback, Amanda strengthened her facility as a coach of her people. Her team became comfortable telling her when she was going too quickly and when she was erring into "keep doing what you're doing" territory. Within a few months, even people who had initially been reticent to receive corrective feedback were checking in with her, unsolicited, to see how they were performing, hungry for more coaching. Leaders in other areas who had previously worked with her people also noticed the changes, gaining Amanda recognition as someone to watch for future career growth.

> *If your actions inspire others to dream more, learn more, do more, and become more, you are a leader.*
> —John Quincy Adams

CHAPTER NINE

Pulling It All Together

A leader's role is to raise people's aspirations for what they can become and to release their energies so they will try to get there.

—David R. Gergen

Congratulations! If you have been using this book as suggested, and taken the time to do all of the exercises and implement all of the suggestions, you have likely gained new insights, increased your level of positivity, and become a more effective coach to your people.

As a result of going through the book, you should now have a pretty good intuitive sense about your strengths and developmental opportunities with respect to being a consummate leader. To consider this topic a little further, however, I encourage you to complete this short self-assessment. As you engage in it, consider your own self-perceptions and reflect on feedback you have received from others, as this can assist you in being objective as you answer the questions.

For each question, rate yourself on a scale of one to five, using the following anchors:

1 – Strongly Disagree
2 – Disagree
3 – Neutral (neither agree nor disagree)
4 – Agree
5 – Strongly Agree

SELF-AWARENESS

1. I can list my top ten strengths. (Give yourself one point for every two strengths you can name up to 10)
2. I can list my top five developmental opportunities. (Give yourself one point for every developmental opportunity you name up to 5)
3. I am aware of the triggers that cause me to behave in undesirable ways.
4. I regularly seek feedback from others.
5. I understand how my upbringing affects my approach to leadership.

SPIRITUALITY

6. I understand how my views about spirituality affect my leadership style.
7. I have a clear sense of purpose in my life.
8. I feel my work aligns with my purpose.
9. I strive to make work meaningful for those around me.
10. If I died tomorrow, I would feel comfortable with the legacy I left.

Self-Management

11. I believe I can improve my skills through hard work and practice.
12. I willingly take on challenges.
13. I take consistent action toward my goals.
14. I maintain a good level of work-life balance, and take time for self-care.
15. I am generally optimistic.

Positivity

16. I am intentional about engaging in behaviors that put me in a positive mood.
17. I consistently find things in my life for which to be grateful.
18. When something does not proceed as planned, I am able to bounce back from it relatively quickly.
19. I regularly use my top character strengths in my work.
20. When interacting with others, I strive to be positive, upbeat, and encouraging.

Authenticity

21. I am able to make myself vulnerable in my interactions with others.
22. I earn my seat at the table by expressing my opinions.
23. I am assertive.
24. My coworkers know the "real" me.
25. I feel comfortable in my own skin.

Positive Relationships

26. I am giving in my interactions with others.
27. I connect with others easily.
28. I listen effectively and strive to understand others' perspectives.
29. I am compassionate.
30. I am intentional about fostering relationships in the workplace.

Coaching and Developing

31. I regularly take time to develop the people who report to me.
32. I frequently give others positive reinforcement for a job well done.
33. I am comfortable providing people with constructive criticism.
34. I believe in the people who report to me.
35. I know the career goals of all my direct reports.

Add up your scores in each area (they will range from 5–25).

Leadership Quality	Score
Self-Awareness	
Spirituality	
Self-Management	
Positivity	
Authenticity	
Positive Relationships	
Coaching and Developing	

Based on a comparison of your scores, you will be able to determine your relative strengths and weaknesses with respect to being a consummate leader.

If all of your scores are relatively low (below 15), you have plenty of opportunities for development. Work your way through the book carefully, conducting all of the exercises. If you have some high scores with some lower ones, be intentional about continuing to leverage your strengths while taking the time to develop in the areas that need work. In both of these scenarios, working with an executive coach can be a way to gain support and an objective outside perspective as you continue to grow and develop.

If all of your scores are relatively high (above 22), congratulations! You are likely a consummate leader. However, if you are a true consummate leader, you realize your development is never complete. Thus, choose the areas on which you scored the lowest, and continue to fine-tune your style so that you can become even more effective.

Reflect on all you have learned about yourself in the process of going through this book, and select one or two development goals on which to work. Even if you have targeted a variety of areas for improvement, I recommend limiting your efforts to one or two goals to start. Taking on more than that may make it difficult for you to focus your efforts enough to really move the needle in terms of your development. As you achieve your goals in one area, you can move onto another area of personal development.

Write down your development goals in your journal as a consistent reminder. Break down each goal into a series of specific, time-based action steps, so you can move toward them in a consistent fashion. Use the people around you for feedback to get a sense of how you are progressing, and make sure you maintain a healthy mindset as you work toward your goal.

Finally, remember that the best leaders are those individuals who are comfortable enough in their own skills and abilities to be willing to regularly self-reflect, take feedback from others, and continue to fine-tune their skills. As John F. Kennedy said, "Leadership and learning are indispensable to each other." Development is a lifelong process, and I encourage you to commit to an ongoing practice so you can maximize your own potential and the growth of those around you. That is what being a consummate leader is all about.

> *I am personally convinced that one person can be a change catalyst, a transformer in any situation, any organization. Such an individual is yeast that can leaven an entire loaf. It requires vision, initiative, patience, respect, persistence, courage, and faith to be a transforming leader.*
>
> —Stephen R. Covey

APPENDIX

LIST OF STRENGTHS

Abstract Thinker
Accountable
Accurate
Achievement-Oriented
Action-Oriented
Adaptable
Agreeable
Ambitious
Analytical
Articulate
Assertive
Attentive
Authoritative
Balanced
Candid
Cautious
Charismatic
Charming
Closer (of Sales)
Collaborative
Common Sense
Compassionate
Competitive
Conceptual
Confident
Conscientious
Considerate
Consistent
Creative
Credible
Critical Thinker
Delegator
Dependable
Detail-Oriented
Determined
Developmentally-Oriented
Diligent
Discerning
Disciplined
Driven
Efficient
Empathetic
Encouraging
Enthusiastic
Entrepreneurial
Even-Keeled
Expressive
Focused
Goal-Oriented
Grounded
Helpful
Humble

- Inclusive
- Independent
- Individualistic
- Industrious
- Influencer
- Ingenious
- Innovative
- Insightful
- Intelligent
- Introspective
- Intuitive
- Judge of Character
- Kind
- Leader
- Listener
- Logical
- Loyal
- Mature
- Methodical
- Nonjudgmental
- Objective
- Open
- Optimistic
- Organized
- Outgoing
- Passionate
- Patient
- Persuasive
- Planner
- Poised
- Polished
- Practical
- Precise
- Predictable
- Proactive
- Process-Oriented
- Project Manager
- Quality-Oriented
- Relationship Builder
- Resilient
- Resourceful
- Respectful
- Responsible
- Results-Oriented
- Self-Aware
- Seller
- Service-Oriented
- Solution-Focused
- Stable
- Steady
- Storyteller
- Strategic
- Supportive
- Tactful
- Tactical
- Tenacious
- Upbeat
- Values-Driven
- Visionary
- Warm

END NOTES

[1] I have had some clients raise their eyebrows when I use the term "developmental opportunities," as they think it is just the "nice psychologist's" euphemism for "weakness." If you choose to think of certain aspects of yourself as a weakness, feel free – I'm all about personal choice! However, I believe that viewing something as an area for development takes away some of the self-judgment and self-criticism associated with it, putting you in a better frame of mind to deal with it productively. See my discussion of Carol Dweck's work in Chapter 3 for further support of this approach.

[2] Saad, L. (2012). U.S. confidence in organized religion at low point. *Gallup Politics,* July.

[3] Summary of Key Findings. (2008). *Statistics on Religion in America Report.* Pew forum on religion and public life.

[4] Peterson, C. & Seligman, M. E. P. (2004). *Character strengths and virtues: A handbook and classification.* New York: Oxford University Press.

[5] Wrzesniewski, A., McCauley, C., Rozin, P. & Schwartz, B. (1997). Jobs, careers, and callings: People's relations to their work, *Journal of Research in Personality, 31,* 21–33.

[6] Wrzesniewski, A. & Dutton, J. E. (2001). Crafting a job: Revisioning employees as active crafters of their work. *The Academy of Management Review, 26*(2), 179–201.

[7] Frankl, V. (2006). *Man's search for meaning.* Boston: Beacon Press, p. 121.

[8] Sy, T., Cote, S. & Saavedra, R. (2005). The contagious leader: Impact of the leader's mood on the mood of group members, group affective tone, and group processes. *Journal of Applied Psychology, 90*(2), 295–305.

[9] Cranston, S. & Keller, S. (2013). Increasing the "Meaning Quotient" of work. *McKinsey Quarterly,* January.

[10] Kray, L. J. & Haselhun, M. P. (2007). Implicit negotiation beliefs and performance: Experimental and longitudinal evidence. *Journal of Personality and Social Psychology, 93*(1), 49–64.

[11] Dweck, C. S. (2006). *Mindset: The new psychology of success.* New York: Random House.

[12] Heslin, P. A., Vandewalle, D. & Latham, G. P. (2006). Keen to help? Managers' implicit person theories and their subsequent employee coaching. *Personnel Psychology, 59,* 871–902.

[13] Wood, R. E. & Bandura, A. (1989). Impact of self-conceptions of ability on self-regulatory mechanisms and complex decision-making. *Journal of Personality and Social Psychology, 56,* 407–415.

[14] Bandura, A. (1977). Self-efficacy: Toward a unifying theory of behavioral change. *Psychological Review, 84,* 191–215.

[15] Bandura, A. (1992). Exercise of personal agency through the self-efficacy mechanisms. In R. Schwarzer (Ed.), *Self-efficacy: Thought control of action.* Washington, DC: Hemisphere.

[16] Seligman, M. (1998). *Learned optimism.* New York: Pocket Books.

[17] Pereira, A. C., Huddleston, D. E., Brickman, A. M., Sosunov, A. A., Hen, R., McKhann, G. M., et al. (2007). An in vivo correlate of exercise-induced neurogenesis in the adult dentate gyrus. *Proceedings of the National Academy of Sciences*, Mar 27; *104*(13), 5638–43.

[18] Ratey, J. J. & Hagerman, E. (2008). *Spark: The revolutionary new science of exercise and the brain.* New York: Little, Brown and Co.

[19] Coulson, J. & McKenna, J. (2005). How does exercising at work influence work performance? A randomised cross-over trial. *Medicine & Science in Sports and Exercise, 37*(5), s323.

[20] Baumeister, R. F. & Tierney, J. (2011). *Willpower: Rediscovering the greatest human strength.* New York: Penguin Press.

[21] Brefczynski-Lewis, J. A., Lutz, A., Schaefer, H. S., Levinson, D. B. & Davidson, R. J. (2007). Neural correlates of attentional expertise in long-term meditation practitioners. Proceedings of the National Academy of Sciences of the United States of America. *104*(27), 11483–11488.

[22] Moyer, C. A., Donnelly, M. P., Anderson, J. C., Valek, K. C., Huckaby, S. J., Widerholt, D. A., Doty, R. L., Rehlinger, A. S. & Rice, B. L. (2011). Frontal electroencephalographic asymmetry associated with positive emotion is produced by very brief meditation training.

[23] Hölzel, B. K., Carmody, J., Vangel, M., Congleton, C., Yerramsetti, S. M., Gard, T. & Lazar, S. W. (2011). Meditation practice leads to increases in regional brain gray matter concentration. *Psychiatry Research: Neuroimaging, 191,* 36–42.

[24] Davidson R. J., Kabat-Zinn, J., Schumacher, J., Rosenkranz, M., Muller, D., Santorelli, S. F., Urbanowski, F., et al. (2003). Alterations in brain and immune function produced by mindfulness meditation. *Psychosomatic Medicine*: Jul–Aug, 65(4), 564–70.

[25] Holzel, B. K., Ott, U., Gard, T., Hempel, H., Weygandt, M., Morgen, K. & Vaitl, D. (2008). Investigation of mindfulness meditation practitioners with voxel-based morphometry. *Social Cognitive and Affective Neuroscience*, 3(1), 55–61.

[26] Tan, C. (2012). *Search inside yourself: The unexpected path to achieving success, happiness (and world peace)*. New York: Harper Collins.

[27] Kabat-Zinn, J. (1994). *Wherever you go, there you are: Mindfulness meditation in everyday life*. New York: Hyperion Books.

[28] Lyubomirsky, S., King, L. & Diener, E. (2005). The benefits of frequent positive affect: Does happiness lead to success? *Psychology Bulletin*, 131(6), 803–855.

[29] Achor, S. (2010). *The happiness advantage: The seven principles of positive psychology that fuel success and performance at work*. New York: Random House.

[30] Baumeister, R. F., Bratslavsky, E., Finkenauer, C. & Vohs, K. D. (2001). Bad is stronger than good. *Review of General Psychology*, 5, 323–370.

[31] Tugend, A. (2012). Why people remember negative events more than positive ones. *The New York Times*. 23 Mar 2012. Retrieved Feb. 26, 2014 from http://www.nytimes.com/2012/03/24/your-money/why-people-remember-negative-events-more-than-positive-ones.html?pagewanted=all

[32] Brown, N. J. L., Sokal, A. D. & Friedman, H. L. (2013). The complex dynamics of wishful thinking: The critical positivity ratio. *American Psychologist, 68*(9), 801–813.

[33] Fredrickson, B. L. (2013). Updated thinking on positivity ratios. *American Psychologist. 60*(7), 678–686.

[34] Keyes, C. L. M. (2002). The mental health continuum: from languishing to flourishing in life. *Journal of Health and Behavior Research, 43*, 207–222.

[35] Fredrickson, B. L. (2001). The role of positive emotions in positive psychology: The broaden-and-build theory of positive emotions. *American Psychologist, 56*, 218–226.

[36] Johnson, L. (2008). *Enjoy life! Healing with happiness: How to harness positive moods to raise your energy, effectiveness, and joy.* Head Acre Publishing.

[37] Lyubomirsky, S., King, L. & Diener, E. (2005). The benefits of frequent positive affect: Does happiness lead to success? *Psychology Bulletin, 131*(6), 803–855.

[38] Robinson, J. (2008). Turning around employee turnover. *Gallup Business Journal*, May.

[39] Sy T., Cote S. & Saavedra, R. (2005). The contagious leader: Impact of the leader's mood on the mood of group members, group affective tone, and group processes. *Journal of Applied Psychology, 90*(2), 295–305.

[40] Barsade, S. G. (2002). The ripple effect: Emotional contagion and its influence on group behavior. *Administrative Science Quarterly. 47*, 644–675.

[41] Rothbard, N. P. & Wilk, S. L. (2011). Waking up on the right or wrong side of the bed: Start-of-workday mood, work events, employee affect, and performance. *Academy of Management Journal, 54*(5), 959–980.

[42] Pugh, S. D. (2001). Service with a smile: Emotional contagion in the service encounter. *Academy of Management Journal, 44*(5), 1018–1027.

[43] Grandey, A. (2003). When "the show must go on": Surface acting and deep acting as determinants of emotional exhaustion and peer-rated service delivery. *Academy of Management Journal, 46*(1), 86–96.

[44] Tugade, M. & Fredrickson, B. (2004). Resilient individuals use positive emotions to bounce back from negative emotional experiences. *Journal of Personality and Social Psychology, 86*(2), 320–333.

[45] Catalino, L. I. & Fredrickson, B. L. (2011). A Tuesday in the life of a flourisher: The role of positive emotional reactivity in optimal mental health. *Emotion, 11*(4), 938–950.

[46] Lyubomirsky, S. (2008). *The how of happiness: A scientific approach to getting the life you want.* New York: Penguin Press.

[47] Stevenson, B. & Wolfers, J. (2013). Subjective well-being and income: Is there any evidence of satiation? *American Economic Review,* American Economic Association, *103*(3), 598–604, May.

[48] Seligman, M. E., Steen, T. A., Park, N. & Peterson, C. (2005). Positive psychology progress: Empirical validation of interventions. *American Psychologist, 60*(5), 410–21.

[49] Lakey, B. (2013). Perceived social support and happiness: The role of personality and relational processes. *Oxford Handbook of Happiness* (Ilona Bondwell Ed.). Oxford: Oxford University Press.

[50] Strack, F., Martin, L. & Stepper, S. (1988). Inhibiting and facilitating conditions of the human smile: A non-obtrusive test of the facial feedback hypothesis. *Journal of Personality and Social Psychology, 54*(5), 768–777.

[51] Manly, R. (2007). Go ahead and smile. *Inside*, January.

[52] Lyubomirsky, S. & Della Porta, M. (2008). Boosting happiness, buttressing resilience: Results from cognitive and behavioral interventions. In J. W. Reich, A. J. Zautra & J. Hall (Eds.), *Handbook of adult resilience: Concepts, methods, and applications.* New York: Guilford Press.

[53] Peterson, C. & Seligman, M. E. P. (2004). *Character strengths and virtues: A handbook and classification.* Oxford: Oxford University Press.

[54] Wood, A. M., Linley, P. A., Matlby, J., Kashdan, T. B. & Hurling, R. (2011). Using personal and psychological strengths leads to increases in well-being over time: A longitudinal study and the development of the strengths use questionnaire. *Personality and Individual Differences, 50*, 15–19.

[55] Harzer, C. & Ruch, W. (2013). The application of signature character strengths and positive experiences at work. *Journal of Happiness Studies. 14*(3), 965–983.

[56] Harzer, C. & Ruch, W. (2012). When the job is a calling: The role of applying one's signature strengths at work. *Journal of Positive Psychology, 7*, 362–371.

[57] Seligman, M. E. P., Steen, T. A., Park, N. & Peterson, C. (2005). Positive psychology progress: Empirical validation of interventions. *American Psychologist, S60*, 410–421.

[58] Fredrickson, B. L. (2013). Updated thinking on positivity ratios. *American Psychologist. 60*(7), 678–686.

[59] Rego, A., Sousa, F., Marques, C. & Cunha, M. P. (2012). Optimism predicting employees' creativity: The mediating role of positive affect and the positivity ratio. *European Journal of Work and Organizational Psychology, 21*(2), 244–270.

[60] Carney, D. R., Hall, J. & Smith LeBeau, L. (2005). Beliefs about the nonverbal expression of social power. *Journal of Nonverbal Behavior, 29*, 105–123.

[61] De Waal, F. (1998). *Chimpanzee politics: Power and sex among apes.* Baltimore: Johns Hopkins University Press.

[62] Carney, D. R., Cuddy, A. J. & Yap, A. J. (2010). Power posing: Brief nonverbal displays affect neuroendocrine levels and risk tolerance. *Psychological Science, 21*(10), 1363–1368.

[63] Cuddy, A. J., Wilmuth, C. A. & Carney, D. R. (2012). The benefit of power posing before a high-stakes social evaluation. *Harvard Business School Working Paper,* 13–027, September.

[64] Bos, M. W. & Cuddy, A. J. C. (2013). iPosture: the size of electronic consumer devices affects our behavior. *Harvard Business School Working Paper,* No. 13–097, May.

[65] Stel, M., van Dijk, E., Smith, P. K., van Dijk, W. W. & Djalal, F. M. (2011). Lowering the pitch of your voice makes you feel more powerful and think more abstractly. *Social Psychological and Personality Science, 3*(4), 497–502.

[66] Lambert, M. J. & Barley, D. E. (2001). Research summary on the therapeutic relationship and psychotherapy outcome. *Psychotherapy: Theory, Research, Practice, Training, 38*(4), 357–361.

[67] Brown, B. (2012). *Daring greatly: How the courage to be vulnerable transforms the way we live, love, parent, and lead.* New York: Gotham.

[68] Cialdini, R. B. (2001). *Influence: Science and practice.* Boston: Allyn & Bacon.

[69] Heilman, M. E., Wallen, A., Fuchs, D. & Tamkins, M. (2004). Penalties for success: Reactions to women who succeed at male gender-typed tasks. *Journal of Applied Psychology, 89*(3), 416–427.

[70] Item 10: I have a best friend at work. *Gallup Business Journal,* 26 May 1999. Retrieved from http://businessjournal.gallup.com/content/511/item-10-best-friend-work.aspx

[71] Carmeli, A., Brueller, D. & Dutton, J. E. (2009). Learning behaviours in the workplace: The role of high-quality interpersonal relationships and psychological safety. *Systems Research and Behavioral Science, 26,* 81–98.

[72] Fredrickson, B. (2013). *Love 2.0: How our supreme emotion affects everything we feel, think, do, and become.* New York: Hudson Street Press.

[73] Ybarra, O., Burnstein, E., Winkielman, P., Keller, M. C., Manis, M., Chan, E. & Rodriguez, J. (2008). Mental exercising through simple socializing: Social interaction promotes general cognitive functioning. *Personality and Social Psychology Bulletin, 34*(2), 248–259.

[74] Grant, A. (2013). *Give and take: A revolutionary approach to success.* New York: Penguin.

[75] Fredrickson, B. (2013). *Love 2.0: How our supreme emotion affects everything we feel, think, do, and become.* New York: Hudson Street Press.

[76] Lyubomirsky, S., King, L. & Diener, E. (2005). The benefits of frequent positive affect: Does happiness lead to success? *Psychology Bulletin, 131*(6), 803–55.

[77] Cabane, O. F. (2012). *The charisma myth: How anyone can master the art and science of personal magnetism.* New York: Penguin.

[78] Lencioni, P. (2012). *The advantage: Why organizational health trumps everything else in business.* San Francisco: Jossey-Bass.

[79] Eden, D. (1990). Leadership and expectations: Pygmalion effects and other self-fulfilling prophecies in organizations. *Leadership Quarterly, 3*(4), 271–305.

[80] Rosenthal, R. & Jacobson, L. (1968). *Pygmalion in the classroom.* New York: Holt, Rinehart & Winston.

[81] Eden, D. (1990). Leadership and expectations: Pygmalion effects and other self-fulfilling prophecies in organizations. *Leadership Quarterly, 3*(4) 271–305.

[82] Babad, E. Y., Inbar, J. & Rosenthal, R. (1982). Pygmalion, Galatea, and the Golem: Investigations of biased and unbiased teachers. *Journal of Educational Psychology, 74,* 459–474.

[83] Boyatzis, R. E., Passarelli, A. P., Koenig, K., Lowe, M., Mathew, B., Stoller, J. & Phillips, M. (2012). Examination of

the neural substrates activated in experiences with resonant and dissonant leaders. *Leadership Quarterly, 23*(2), 259–272.

[84] Jack, A. I., Boyatzis, R. E., Khawaja, M. S., Passarelli, A. M. & Leckie, R. L. (2013). Visioning in the brain: An fMRI study of inspirational coaching and mentoring. *Social Neuroscience, 8*(4), 369–84.

[85] Boyatzis, R. (2011). Neuroscience and leadership: The promise of insights. *Ivey Business Journal*, January–February.

RECOMMENDED READING & VIEWING ON NUTRITION, EXERCISE & MEDITATION

Bittman, Mark. *Food Matters: A Guide to Conscious Eating.* New York: Simon & Schuster, 2009.

Carr, Kris. *Crazy Sexy Diet.* New York: skirt! 2011.

Food, Inc. DVD. Directed by Robert Kenner. Magnolia Home Entertainment, 2009.

Food Matters. DVD. Directed by James Colquhoun & Laurentine ten Bosch. 2009.

Hungry for Change. DVD. Directed by James Colquhoun, Laurentine ten Bosch & Carlo Ledesma. 2012.

Hutchinson, Alex. *Which Comes First, Cardio or Weights?* New York: William Morrow, 2011.

Kabat-Zinn, Jon. *Wherever You Go, There You Are.* New York: Hyperion, 2005.

O'Connell, Jeff. *Sugar Nation: The Hidden Truth Behind America's Deadliest Habit and the Simple Way to Beat It.* New York: Hyperion, 2011.

Reno, Tosca. *The Eat Clean Cookbook.* New York: Ballantine, 2007.

Roizen, Michael F. and Mehmet C. Oz. *You: The Owner's Manual.* New York: William Morrow, 2013.

Stiles, Tara. *Yoga Cures.* New York: Three Rivers Press, 2012.

Tan, Chade-Meng. *Search Inside Yourself: The Unexpected Path to Achieving Success, Happiness (and World Peace).* New York: HarperCollins, 2012.

ACKNOWLEDGEMENTS

This book was a definite labor of love that was several years in the making, and I have so many people I would like to thank. First, I am truly thankful for my parents Lloyd and Eva Thompson for their enthusiastic support my whole life, and for their willing and encouraging proofreading from the early stages of this project through to the very end. Thanks also to my husband, Markeal, who instead of expressing dismay that I decided to have a baby, become an entrepreneur, and write a book all in the same year, urged me to go after my dreams. To my son, Blake, whose upbeat spirit and bright smile always reminds me not to take myself too seriously, thank you. I am also deeply grateful to my sisters, Maria and Alicia, and my brother, Terry, for encouraging my artistic endeavors from early on. Kiana, Malcolm, and Justin, thank you for inspiring me through your bright eyes, positivity, and curiosity.

Thank you to my editor and book designer, Stacey Aaronson. Your facility with the English language, artistic eye, and creativity were instrumental in putting together such a polished book. Your encouragement and enthusiasm also helped me to deal with some of the vulnerability I felt as a first-time author since I knew that, with your help, I would be able to publish a book of which I could be very proud.

Professionally, I would like to express heartfelt thanks to Gary Sperduto for his mentoring and the belief he showed in me as I pursued this project. To all the clients I worked with across the years from whom I learned so much, thank you for your trust and for sharing your insights and wisdom with me.

In addition, I would like to express sincere thanks to Adam Rifkin and Adam Grant who, purely out of the kindness of their hearts, assisted me as I was going through the publishing process. They are true givers, and proof that contrary to what some would have you believe, there are generous people in the world.

Thank you also to Chris Yeh, whose wonderful foreword added so much to this book. I am sincerely humbled to have received such kind words from someone as accomplished as you. I would also like to express genuine gratitude to Marshall Goldsmith for your wonderful endorsement. I deeply appreciate that you took the time to do that for me. Also, to the amazing Nadine Kaslow, without whom I never would have even known what corporate psychology was, thanks for playing such an important role in my career development.

To Rich Hua, Pat Daniels, Barry Blakley, Daniel Crosby, Karen Watts, Joslyn Gordon, and Ron Kellman who read the manuscript and provided such uplifting words of encouragement, thank you for your time, energy, and willingness to help me.

To my colleagues – especially Dale Belles, Chris Reilly, Kay Loerch, and Becky Winkler, thank you for challenging me, teaching me, and entertaining me over the years.

Thanks to my other cheerleaders along the way – Matthew Simmons, Brett Peavy, and Michelle Ripple. It really is a wonderful feeling to have friends in my corner supporting my literary efforts. Also, to Linda, Kerry, and Douglas Bair, thanks for being my partners in crime over the years in our various sublime and ridiculous endeavors that contributed to the development of my creative gifts. To Erica Bracey, thank you so much for your ideas and assistance. I have learned so much through my work with you.

Finally, thank you to various people who (sometimes unwittingly and inadvertently) taught me about my own strengths and talents and were catalysts for growth: Phillippe, Scott, Adena, Derek, and Janet.

ABOUT THE AUTHOR

D R. PATRICIA THOMPSON is an award-winning teacher, researcher, and corporate psychologist who has consulted to senior executives since 2004. On the way to earning her PhD in Clinical Psychology, she was educated at the University of Toronto, Georgia State University, The University of Pennsylvania, and the Emory School of Medicine. She currently teaches corporations and individuals how to leverage the science of positive psychology to enhance their personal and professional results, believing that a holistic approach that addresses one's body, mind, and spirit is the key to achieving peak performance in a variety of domains. She lives in Atlanta, GA, with her husband, Markeal, and son, Blake.

www.patricia-thompson.com

www.ingramcontent.com/pod-product-compliance
Lightning Source LLC
Chambersburg PA
CBHW051942290426
44110CB00015B/2077